GILDING

the

COUCAL

From his Mother's Arms
to
Lieutenant Commander
1930 to 1974

JAMES W. GIBSON

Edited by George Winship

To: Dana with Warm Regards! 4-6-21
Lcdr James W. Gibson USN (Ret)

GILDING THE COUCAL

ISBN 978-0-9994647-2-4

Printed in USA by 48HrBooks (www.48HrBooks.com)

Dedication

To those submariners now living
and those on eternal patrol.

Acknowledgments

Thanks to my loving wife Mary Lou.
Without her constant help
none of this would have happened.

Thanks also to
Vice Admiral James Wilson
Rear Admiral Randy Moore
Captain Herbert O. Burton
Captain Jerry J. Nuss
Captain James Varley
Captain James Patton
Captain Mike Tiernan
Commander Peter Fawcett
Captain Barney Barnett
LCDR Jimmy Gee
Dominic Boncore
Norman Hosking
Paul Berry

Table of Contents

Foreword by Herbert O. Burton 1

Chapter 1: First Impressions 3

Chapter 2: Settling In 6

Chapter 3: Taking Inventory 8

Chapter 4: Accepting the Challenge 10

Chapter 5: Mind Your Ps and B 12

Chapter 6: Captain on the Bridge 14

Chapter 7: Pennsylvania Roots 16

Chapter 8: Dad, Mom and Me 18

Chapter 9: Faith and Service 20

Chapter 10: Great Depression 23

Chapter 11: Uncle William Douglas 25

Chapter 12: Day of Infamy 26

Chapter 13: First Job 28

Chapter 14: Traps, Pelts and Skunks 29

Chapter 15: Earning $1 per Hour 30

Chapter 16: Baseball with Honus Wagner 32

Chapter 17: Top to Bottom 34

Chapter 18: Selected for Command 37

Chapter 19: Deep Diving School 39

Chapter 20: Warmed Over Death 41

Chapter 21: Protecting My Candy Ass 42

Chapter 22: Saving the Tree 45

Chapter 23: Take Your Bubbles With You 46

Chapter 24: Managing Buoyancy 47

Chapter 25: Walking on Eggshells 49

Chapter 26: Averting Disaster 51

Chapter 27: Mary Lou to the Rescue 53

Chapter 28: Sinking a Destroyer 55

Chapter 29: Working Nights and Weekends 57

Chapter 30: Blood, Sweat and Tears 58

Chapter 31: Fast Cruising 59

Chapter 32: Engineman School 61

Chapter 33: Climbing a Fence 63

Chapter 34: Fireman Apprentice 65

Chapter 35: Submarine School 66

Chapter 36: Momsen's Lung 67

Chapter 37: First Submarine Ride 69

Chapter 38: Dirty Laundry; Dirty Tricks 70

Chapter 39: Time for Fishing 72

Chapter 40: Boosting Morale 74

Chapter 41: Paybacks are Hell! 76

Chapter 42: Personal Touch 78

Chapter 43: Transversing the Isthmus 82

Chapter 44: Hot Bunking on the *Conger* 84

Chapter 45: Getting Qualified 86

Chapter 46: Non-Combatant 88

Chapter 47: Engineman Duties 89

Chapter 48: Learning a Lesson 91

Chapter 49: Humor in Uniform 93

Chapter 50: Another Lesson Learned 95

Chapter 51: Hot Shot! 97

Chapter 52: Getting Qualified Redux 99

Chapter 53: Wetting My Dolphins 100

Chapter 54: Atlantic Coast Duty 102

Chapter 55: Time Out for Sports 104

Chapter 56: Underway Training 106

Chapter 57: Rescue Missions 109

Chapter 58: Kudos to the *Coucal* 111

Chapter 59: Medical Emergency 115

Chapter 60: Armed Forces Day Parade 116

Chapter 61: Special Ops in the Arctic North 118

Chapter 62: Diesel Fumes and Oil Stains 120

Chapter 63: California Bound 121

Chapter 64: Casting the Leads 123

Chapter 65: Horse and Cow 125

Chapter 66: Back on the Gridiron 127

Chapter 67: Moonlighting for C&H Sugar 129

Chapter 68: Time to Re-Enlist 131

Chapter 69: Chance Encounter 134

Chapter 70: Fate Steps In 136

Chapter 71: Mary Louise Buckthought 137

Chapter 72: Allure of a Convertible 138

Chapter 73: Whirlwind Romance 140

Chapter 74: Sea Trials on the *Bass* 141

Chapter 75: Permission Granted 143

Chapter 76: Hawaii, Here We Come 145

Chapter 77: Sand Castles and Motel Rooms 147

Chapter 78: Playing Tourist 150

Chapter 79: Flying on *Marina Mars* 151

Chapter 80: Visiting Relatives 153

Chapter 81: Managing the Fleet 154

Chapter 82: On the Mound 156

Chapter 83: Sailing Vessels 158

Chapter 84: Sick Leave and Paperwork 160

Chapter 85: Expecting Our First Child 162

Chapter 86: A Goal Worth Chasing 164

Chapter 87: Stay or Play 165

Chapter 88: War Story 166

Chapter 89: Jumping Ship 168

Chapter 90: Bugler's Call 170

Chapter 91: On the Picket Line 174

Chapter 92: Mixing Oil and Sea Water 176

Chapter 93: Engine Repair 178

Chapter 94: Just Desserts 180

Chapter 95: Third Lesson Learned 181

Chapter 96: Going Nuclear 183

Chapter 97: Making Ends Meet 185

Chapter 98: Hunter's Paradise 188

Chapter 99: Instructing Legends 190

Chapter 100: Going AWOL 194

Chapter 101: Witty Repartee 196

Chapter 102: Jumping Ladders 197

Chapter 103: Starting Over 199

Chapter 104: Survivor's Remorse 201

Chapter 105: Officer and a Gentleman 203

Chapter 106: Qualifying as an Officer 205

Chapter 107: Guide to Pink Elephants 207

Chapter 108: Herbert O. Burton 209

Chapter 109: My Man Finch 211

Chapter 110: Diving Solo 214

Chapter 111: Starry, Starry Night 217

Chapter 112: Custom Tailored 219

Chapter 113: Ready for Qualification 220

Chapter 114: Dolphins Get Wet Again 222

Chapter 115: Through Sickness and Health 224

Chapter 116: Crown of Thorns 226

Chapter 117: Scourge of the Sea Bat 229

Chapter 118: Complete Turnaround 231

Chapter 119: Plebe Orientation 233

Chapter 120: Friendship versus Professionalism . 234

Chapter 121: What is Your Call Sign? 236

Chapter 122: Ship in Distress 238

Chapter 123: Shopping Cart Races 239

Chapter 124: Finch Strikes Again 241

Chapter 125: Snake Ranch Christmas 243

Chapter 126: Stay-at-Home Mom 244

Chapter 127: Speedy Diet Plan 245

Chapter 128: Overcome by Smoke 247

Chapter 129: Rubbing Shoulders With Stars 248

Chapter 130: Flying submariner 252

Chapter 131: Cooper River Desk Job 256

Chapter 132: Blue and Gold Coordinator 258

Chapter 133: Field of Dreams 260

Chapter 134: Gibson Field Commendation 263

Chapter 135: Extended Road Trip 265

Chapter 136: Unexpected Problems 267

Chapter 137: Dry Dock Refueling Test 269

Chapter 138: Deep Knee Pain 271

Chapter 139: Take the *Hake* for Knee Relief 273

Chapter 140: Winning the Nimitz Trophy 275

Chapter 141: Small Ship Training Officer 277

Chapter 142: City of Brotherly Love 278

Chapter 143: Sounding the Alarm 280

Chapter 144: Pennsylvania Crude 282

Chapter 145: After-Hours Research 284

Chapter 146: Monumental Climb 286

Chapter 147: Sailing First Class 288

Chapter 148: Career on the Line 290

Chapter 149: Carrot, Stick and Falcon 294

Chapter 150: Inquiry and Intrigue 297

Chapter 151: Under Investigation 299

Chapter 152: Classified Assignment 300

Chapter 153: En Route to WestPac 302

Chapter 154: Cold War Spy Craft 304

Chapter 155: Visit to Saipan 307

Chapter 156: Mystery of ChiChi Jima 310

Chapter 157: Shopping Therapy 312

Chapter 158: A Close Call 314

Chapter 159: Navigating by Braille 316

Chapter 160: Mystic Hong Kong 318

Chapter 161: Land of the Morning 321

Chapter 162: Mary Sou's Girls 323

Chapter 163: Navy Achievement Medal 325

Chapter 164: Return to Pearl 327

Chapter 165: Relinquishing Command 329

Chapter 166: Kudos All Around 335

Chapter 167: Old Man and the Sea 337

Chapter 168: Standing Watch 339

Chapter 169: Meritorious Service Medal 341

Chapter 170: Navy Recruiting Officer 346

Chapter 171: Puppy Smuggling 348

Chapter 172: Making a Name for the Navy 349

Chapter 173: Epilogue 352

Afterword by Dominic Boncore 354

Foreword by Herbert O. Burton

I was shipmates with James Gibson on the *USS Pomfret* (SS 391) in the early 1960s. He was a newly commissioned Ensign in a Navy program that allowed outstanding senior enlisted personnel to be commissioned as Limited Duty Officer.

Jim had qualified for submarine duty as an enlisted member and made sure we knew he intended to re-qualify as a submarine officer, which he did. He joined a wardroom consisting of officers commissioned from the US Naval Academy and the US Navy Reserve Training Corps and was exposed initially to some uncomfortable moments.

But he was not affected. He only worked harder and quicker to qualify for the golden dolphins.

He and I lived some distance from the berth of the *Pomfret* but in relatively close neighborhoods so we shared car pooling. After one or the other of us transferred, we lost contact.

I next heard of LCDR Gibson from another officer with whom I served. This officer was a once removed Commanding Officer of the *USS Catfish* (SS-339) from the time period when Gibson was in her crew. He proclaimed that the former Commanding Officer and he had each reaped the rewards of Jim's hard work, tenacity and professionalism.

It was well known throughout the submarine force that the *Catfish* had gone from an unsatisfactory condition to an almost unbelievable improvement during Gibson's tour onboard and being in charge of several different departments. I happily indicated that I too had served with this outstanding officer.

As a newly commissioned Lieutenant Commander, Gibson continued his professional ambition and was designated Qualified for Command. He was now assigned duty as the Commanding Officer of the *USS Coucal* (ASR-8).

I next encountered him when he and the *Coucal* had deployed to the Western Pacific (WestPac). As a Commanding Officer, Jim was making a call on the Commander Seventh Fleet.

During his call, Jim was asked several questions regarding current operations by units of the Soviet Navy in the vicinity of Guam. LCDR Gibson's ship had surveyed that area during their transit to WestPac and he provided the Admiral with a firsthand evaluation of that situation.

Later I was advised by the Admiral that he was most impressed with the report and with the presence of LCDR Gibson.

So my personal knowledge of LCDR Gibson spans the circuit from a newly commissioned Ensign in the Limited Duty Officer Program to Lieutenant Commander and the Commanding Officer of an ASR. LCDR Gibson was highly praised by the Commander of the Seventh Fleet and several commands.

He has demonstrated professionalism, dedication and continued involvement throughout his entire Navy career.

In retirement, he continues to provide these same attributes. His contributions are reflected in the attention to the Submariner community in his retirement area.

It has been my personal pleasure to have known him and I have always admired his intense drive to make things better.

Herb Burton
Captain, US Navy (Retired)
North Carolina

Chapter 1

First Impressions

"I can imagine no more rewarding a career. And any man who may be asked in this century what he did to make his life worthwhile, I think can respond with a good deal of pride and satisfaction:
I served in the United States Navy."
President John F. Kennedy
August 1, 1963
Bancroft Hall, graduation ceremony
US Naval Academy

My first real glimpse of the *USS Coucal* (ASR-8) was in the Pearl Harbor shipyard shortly after I arrived in Hawaii as her newly assigned skipper.

A once proud *Chanticleer*-class submarine rescue vessel, her keel had been laid down on September 30, 1941, at the Moore Dry Dock Company in Oakland, California. She was launched May 29, 1942, and commissioned into service by the US Navy on January 22, 1943, with Lieutenant Commander David H. Byerly as her first skipper.

During World War II, the *Coucal* had been assigned to patrol the Asiatic-Pacific theatre and even saw some action in Europe in support of Allied submarines operating in those waters.

USS Coucal in dry dock, Pearl Harbor, HI

Between 1945 and 1951, the *Coucal* and her various crews had earned two Navy Occupation Service medals in Asia, another in Europe and a China Service Medal (Extended) during a nearly two-month posting there.

However, when I first saw her in 1969, she was well past her glory days and in the final throes of a complete overhaul after returning from a six-month tour in the Western Pacific.

Named for a family of 30 species of birds in the cuckoo family, the *USS Coucal* was the second in a series of five submarine rescue ships — *Chanticleer, Coucal, Florikan, Greenlet* and *Macaw* — built by the Moore Shipyards.

South American Coucal

4

By the time I first saw her, the *USS Coucal*, through no fault of its own, had acquired a terrible reputation. There were stories that the ship should have been towed back to Pearl Harbor from Yokosuka, Japan, because of the terrible shape she was in.

It seemed that every time the *Coucal* was laid up in port for scheduled routine maintenance, something would come up.

Repeatedly, the ship would be half-fixed or partly torn apart and the powers at be would get her underway in that condition. Maintenance was quite often put aside leaving the long-neglected ship to suffer and limp along.

Eventually, the ship would be patched together enough to continue her duties, but it had been a long time since the *Coucal* had been fully serviceable.

Chapter 2

Settling In

For these and other reasons, the *Coucal* had earned a bad reputation in the Pacific Ocean's Seventh Fleet at the various ports of call including at several US Navy shipyards. However, those decisions by the command staff and the lack of attention from its skipper and crew were never mentioned when those same powers that be were bad-mouthing the *Coucal*.

I knew from the research I had done on her from Navy records that she displaced 1,780 tons, was 251 feet and 4 inches from stem to stern, carried a beam of 42 feet and drafted 14 feet, 3 inches.

When working properly, her four Alco 539 Diesel main engines driving four General Electric generators were coupled with a single Westinghouse main reduction gear producing 3,000 shaft horse power to a single propeller.

All this was music to my ears because I had originally trained as an Engineman right out of basic training.

Although her top speed was nominally rated at 14 knots, a more leisurely 9 knots was her normal cruising speed I quickly was to learn from practical experience.

I knew the *Coucal* could comfortably carry a crew of six commissioned officers and 96 enlisted men around the world, as she had ably demonstrated during World War II, just as long as her fuel tanks, containing 74,970 gallons of diesel, were topped off regularly.

Having seen her share of warfare, the *Coucal* had once carried a full complement of light armament, including two single 3-inch or 50 caliber dual-purpose gun mounts, eight 20-millimeter Anti-Aircraft gun mounts and four depth charge tracks.

By the time I joined up with her, however, most of those weapons had since been removed and the deck space converted to the ship's peace-time missions of submarine rescue.

My off hours during this dry dock period were spent finding a place for my family to live while I was at sea. Even though I was somewhat familiar with Oahu and Pearl Harbor from previous stays there, I received a lot of help from friends in other squadrons. Very quickly, through their efforts, I was able to rent a comfortable home in the Little Makalopa neighborhood, up the hill and across the Kam Highway from the Pearl Harbor Submarine Base.

Our home had a beautiful view of the entire base and I could see the *USS Coucal* waiting for me down below, even if it was some distance away.

Chapter 3

Taking Inventory

The *Coucal* was in the shipyard completing the final days of an overhaul after returning from a six-month Western pacific (WestPac) tour.

During the weeks of repair leading up to my taking command, I spent many hours on the barge going through all of the ship's records, classified documents and orders. I made an inventory of all the paperwork and signed for all of the classified documents. The *Coucal* was not occupied during the repair work being done on board, so all of the ship's commissioned officers and enlisted chiefs met on the barge each day to take care of port duties.

I garnered some sense of the morale problems amongst the crew simply by watching the officers at work on the barge and how they interacted with their skipper. I could tell the officers were all walking on eggshells.

The skipper would come in each morning and issue his orders, then he would go up to the Officers Club on base for lunch.

When the skipper returned to the barge several hours later, he would change his previous orders.

I also got a feel for the morale because somebody told me during that transition period that no one had re-enlisted on board the *USS Coucal* during the past four years, whether by a first-termer or guys that had done 10 years in the Navy. The sailors that did re-enlist had all transferred to somewhere else and then re-enlisted there. That told me a lot about the morale issues right there.

All of this was going through my head as I approached the gangway of the ship with a few of the other officers I had invited to the ship's Change of Command ceremony on Oct. 12, 1969.

Suddenly, from high above me, I distinctly heard a shout, "Boy, Jim, I sure am glad you got here."

To this day, I have no idea who gave that greeting.

I do remember, however, that the previous skipper muttered under his breath, "That sailor is an asshole!"

At the Change of Command ceremony, there were probably 30 people there, including 18 of my friends and three members of my own family — my wife Mary Lou and our two boys — whom I had invited.

I wore my dress whites with my ceremonial sword dangling from a sash tied around my waist.

As I looked around, however, I noticed there were few others present, especially those from the base command headquarters located just up on the hill. That indicated to me a level of contempt held for the previous commander and the *Coucal* at large.

Something would have to change quickly, and I would need to figure that out pronto.

Moments later, during the brief ceremony, I addressed the ship's Commanding Officer with the words "I relieve you, sir."

Chapter 4

Accepting the Challenge

"I believe it is the duty of every man to act as though the fate of the World depends on them.
Surely, no one man can do it all.
But one man CAN make a difference."

Admiral Hyman G. Rickover

During the Change of Command ceremony, Jim Kennedy, the Division Commander made the following statement, "It is hoped that Lieutenant Commander Gibson can bring the *Coucal* back to be a unit in the Pacific Submarine Force that we all can be proud of."

I took his words to be a challenge, but I imagine it was very embarrassing for the other skipper and his crew members present to hear.

Lt. Cmdr. James Gibson takes command

I will never forget that moment as long as I live, watching as that poor skipper was having to eat those words.

Fortunately, the ship's previous Commanding Officer did have extensive prior experience as a Navy Shipyard Superintendent. He had arranged to have the *Coucal* put through an exceptional and professional shipyard overhaul. Thus, the ship left to my command was in an excellent state of repair.

The Change of Command ceremony went off as planned. A short time later, the ship's officers and assembled guests gathered at the submarine officer's club in Lockwood Hall for a taste of champagne or other drinks to celebrate.

All went well until the *Coucal*'s Engineering Officer reported to me that the ship was on fire.

Immediately, the previous skipper turned to me and said, "You've got the command!"

A few tense moments followed, but before too long we were informed that an alert duty officer keeping watch on board the *Coucal* was able to take charge of the situation. As it turned out, the fire was deemed not too serious. The burned area was quickly repaired and the ship's remaining overhaul was completed on time.

During the remaining repair period, it became my task to cause the ordering and organizing of all the supplies necessary for getting the *USS Coucal* underway once the ship was deemed safe to leave dry dock.

Those tasks seemed so rudimentary, but that is what you did as a Captain.

Chapter 5

Mind Your Ps and B

This is as good a place as any to insert a poem presented to me by Admiral John Hyland, then Commander in Chief of the United States Pacific Fleet:

Command at Sea

The Prestige, Privilege and Burden of Command

Only a seaman realizes to what extent an entire ship reflects the personality and ability of one individual, her Commanding Officer. To a landsman, this is not understandable, and sometimes it is even difficult for us to comprehend, — but it is so.

A ship at sea is a distant world in herself and, in consideration of the protracted and distant operations of the fleet units, the Navy must place great power, responsibility and trust in the hands of those leaders chosen for command.

In each ship there is one man who, in the hour of emergency or peril at sea, can turn to no other person. There is one alone who is ultimately responsible for the safe navigation, engineering performance, accurate gun-firing and morale of his ship.
He is the Commanding Officer. He is the ship.

This is the most difficult and demanding assignment in the Navy. There is not an instant during his tour of duty as Commanding Officer that he can escape the grasp of command responsibility. His privileges, in view of his obligations, are most ludicrously small. Nevertheless, command is the spur which has given the Navy its great leaders.

It is a duty which most richly deserves the highest time-honored title of the seafaring world — CAPTAIN.

Chapter 6

Captain on the Bridge

"A captain of the Navy ought to be a man of strong and well-connected sense, with a tolerable good education as well as a seaman, both in theory and practice."

John Paul Jones
Naval Commander
American Revolutionary War

After a couple weeks filled with many tests and trials, we departed the shipyard and returned to the Pearl Harbor Submarine Base. A short upkeep period then followed until we departed the Submarine Base for the *Coucal*'s first underway period under my command.

Once we cleared the entrance of Pearl Harbor and were safely at sea, I turned the ship over to the Officer of the Deck and went below to my stateroom. There, I changed into my khakis or underway uniform, then I returned to the bridge.

As I entered the pilot house, the Boatswain Mate of the Watch shouted, "Captain on the Bridge."

Startled, I turned around to see to whom he might be referring. Somewhat chagrined, I realized he was announcing my presence.

Now that we were underway, I decided it was time to test the crew's training to determine just how weak it might be.

I ordered the Boatswain Mate of the Watch to collect an empty five-gallon coffee can from the Crew's Mess and toss it over the side. Once it hit the water, I ordered him to shout, "Man overboard!"

Upon hearing the shout, the Officer of the Deck immediately turned to me and said, "Captain how do you want me to pick him up?"

I was completely taken aback at this lack of what should have been a routine procedure!

I then told him in very harsh terms, "Just get the man back on board and we will talk about it later."

I was shocked to learn that the crew was not familiar with several prescribed methods for retrieving a man that is overboard. I also wondered what the Officer of the Deck's response and actions might have been if I had not been present on the bridge.

After several days of underway training and many more "man overboard" drills, the ship was ordered to Lahaina Roads by the island of Maui for deep diver training.

It quickly dawned on me that assuming command of any group of individuals was, in many ways, like being adopted into a family. That was a concept familiar to me. This realization brought floods of early childhood memories into my mind whenever I was allowed time to relax and reflect in my stateroom.

Chapter 7

Pennsylvania Roots

"The joys of parents are secret, and so are their griefs and fears."

Sir Francis Bacon
English philosopher (1561-1620)
Essays, 'Of Marriage and Single Life'

I was adopted while a small infant, before my first birthday on May, 29, 1931, by Samuel and Sarah Belle Gibson, residents of Mount Jackson, Pennsylvania.

Two years previous, Samuel and Sarah Belle had welcomed into the world a baby son of their own that they christened Robert. But Robert contracted pneumonia the next year and died before his first birthday.

This was a crushing and devastating blow for the Gibson's, but especially for Sam. The doctors informed him that his wife Sarah Belle would no longer be able to bear any more children.

That is when Mom and Dad decided to adopt me.

I was born in nearby Lebanon, Penn., but I know of no other details regarding my biological parents other than they had placed me for adoption.

Samuel and Sarah Belle took me in and no child could ever have more loving and caring parents. Together we weathered several storms such as appendicitis and other childhood maladies.

Historians called this period the Great Depression. But Sam and Sarah Belle had wisely built a house in Mount Jackson at the start of 1929, well before the stock markets crashed.

Throughout the Great Depression, my parents struggled to maintain that house as a comfortable home for the three of us. They did this through great sacrifice and very hard work.

Dad not only worked long hours, but every year he planted a very large garden.

Jimmy Gibson, 3

Mom canned most of the garden produce so we could enjoy it through much of the year. My earliest memories of childhood include the sights, sounds and smells of her canning 100 quarts of tomatoes and 100 quarts of peaches because "Little Jimmie liked them."

Many other kinds of vegetables met a similar fate.

When it came to food, Mom spoiled me rotten.

By today's standards, most of our meals were hearty, calorie-laden feasts. Sarah Belle was a stay-at-home Mom even though she had a teacher's certificate from both Ohio and Pennsylvania.

She worked tirelessly to make our home a wonderful place in which to be raised.

Chapter 8

Dad, Mom and Me

Dad had worked as a superintendent of the Lake Erie Limestone Company in Hillsville, Penn., until the Depression came along.

Suddenly, there wasn't any more work at that company.

He went from a fine-paying position to a menial laborer's job at Burton Powder, a dynamite producing company later acquired by American Cyanamid, a firm located in Edinburgh, Penn., not far from our home.

Mom and Dad struggled to made ends meet. Even as a young lad, I was aware of their struggles. Nevertheless, I was always well-clothed, well-fed and cared for with great love and tenderness.

Samuel, James and Sarah Belle Gibson

In 1936, however, Sarah Belle was diagnosed in a serious stage of diabetes. Mom loved sweets and so did Dad. When the diagnosis was made, my Dad put down the law that there would be no more sweets made in our house.

In a few years, saccharin became a popular sugar substitute, especially during World War II when sugar was scarce due to rationing. However, I never grew accustomed to its taste.

Mom took good care of herself and endured the ritual shot of insulin each morning.

Like other diabetics, she suffered mood swings. Through perseverance, hard work and a strict diet, she lived to the age of 70.

Chapter 9

Faith and Service

"Fight the good fight of faith, lay hold on eternal life to which you were also called and have confessed the good confession in the presence of many witnesses."

Holy Bible, I Timothy
Chapter 6, Verse 12
New King James Version

Our family of three attended the Westfield Presbyterian Church near Mount Jackson.

The church was named Westfield because a parishioner had donated his west field to the community for construction of a church and cemetery. The earliest grave there dates back to 1803.

Dad, Mom and I participated in most church events. During the Great Depression, everybody made their own entertainment. Most of our family's free time revolved around the church and the local American Legion Post.

The church frequently held fish fry gatherings, hosted Sunday school picnics and produced special programs on Christmas and Easter for the entire community to enjoy. We kids were in most of those programs.

The Earl J. Watt American Legion Post, Number 638, was established first in Enon Valley, Penn., and later moved to Mount

Jackson. It was very popular in our community and the surrounding area.

Dad had served as a mule skinner with the 332nd Infantry of the US Army during World War I and saw action in both Italy and France. He drove a six-mule team hitch and pulled a kitchen vehicle during the war.

Dad and Mom were both deeply involved in the local American Legion Post. Dad served as Post Commander several times and Mom worked with the Ladies Auxiliary of the Post.

At first, the Post held meetings in the old high school building on the west side of town. Later, after the school was consolidated into a larger district, they converted the former high school building

Samuel Gibson, World War I

into a Legion Hall. That is where I remember the Legion Post held square dances and parties, besides holding all of their own Legion meetings.

I and the other Legionnaire kids would play together during the meetings.

Also, as an offshoot of the Legion post's activities, there were often card parties organized for games of Rook or 500. These were held at the homes of Legion members.

Chapter 10

Great Depression

Things were surely different when compared to today. People were poor during the Great Depression, but they always seemed to make the best of their bad situations. Everyone shared what they could to help each other out.

I learned at a young age that my Dad would do almost anything I asked of him. He would give me anything if it was in his power to do so.

Once, at a Legion function, I wanted to buy something so I asked Dad for a quarter. He turned to me and said, "Jim, I don't have a quarter."

Another strong memory of that period in my early years was Decoration Day, now called Memorial Day.

When I was still a small boy, my Dad and I would get into his 1928 Chevy on Decoration Day and we would drive to different cemeteries to place flags on each veteran's grave. I remember this was done in a very reverent manner with few, if any, words.

I grew up knowing that we should honor those deceased veterans who paid the ultimate price for our freedom and way of life. There were no three-day holidays back then. Decoration Day was always held on May 30, no matter when it fell during the week.

Listening to the radio was another big event for our family. I remember enjoying broadcasts of the Pittsburgh Pirates baseball games, especially those with play-by-play action announced by Rosy Roswell, a distant cousin of mine

We also listened to the radio for programs such as *Mr. District Attorney*. And Mom rarely missed the radio antics of Ma Perkins.

Chapter 11

Uncle William Douglas

Other strong memories of those growing up years include those of my uncle William J. Douglas. Uncle Will, as I knew him, owned a small farm about five miles distant near the little town of Enon Valley. I spent many days on that farm, mostly getting in the way of my Uncle Will.

This was during a time when you could still make a living on 40 acres with six or seven cows, a few pigs, chickens and a very large garden. Spending time on that farm was a great learning experience for me.

I saw and sometimes participated in hand milking the cows or feeding the hogs. As I grew older, I was allowed to operate a small farm tractor that Uncle Will owned.

By the age of 12, I had also learned to drive Uncle Will's Model A Ford around the farm.

However, my Uncle Will's baseball prowess fascinated me more than did anything else about him or the farm. When Will was young, he was a very accomplished baseball pitcher and he spent hours teaching me the basics. His brother Tom, a catcher, was also a very good athlete. If fact, the Pittsburgh Pirates tried as best they could to place those two brothers under contract. However, my uncles refused to play baseball on Sundays.

Tragically, Uncle Will died in a farm accident in 1946.

Chapter 12

Day of Infamy

On Sunday, December 7, 1941, the Japanese launched a surprise attack on the American military facilities at Pearl Harbor on the island of Oahu in the Hawaiian Islands. Many people my age can still remember where they were on that fateful day.

Dad, Mom and I were visiting with my Uncle Carson and his family in McMurray, Penn.

My cousin Leroy Zimmerman had just received his pilot's license and had taken me for my very first airplane ride in a two-seat Piper Cub. I recall we flew out of an airport near Canonsburg.

Canonsburg was then home to the well-known singer Perry Como. Back then, Mr. Como operated a barbershop. In fact, locals knew him as "the singing barber." For quite a few years, Mr. Como's barbershop was where some of my mother's relatives received their haircuts.

I vividly remember radio station KDKA announcers in Pittsburgh interrupting regular programming to announce the Japanese sneak attack in and around the Pearl Harbor Navy Base and on several other military areas on the Island of Oahu.

What had started as a joyous day aloft in an airplane quickly became a very solemn day filled with the sobs of women crying and men predicting how long the war would likely last.

There was little known, if anything, about the Hawaiian Islands or, for that matter, the Pacific Ocean. No one in our circle of friends had any idea where Pearl Harbor was, or for that matter what and where was the Island of Oahu.

Remember, those were the days of very limited communications, well before the days of television. Our news back then was gained primarily from word-of-mouth. Newspapers were mostly found in the big cities. Moreover, radio, a very new device, had been on the air for only 10 years or less.

Chapter 13

First Job

As World War II progressed, I turned 13 and went to work for a wonderful farmer by the name of Bill Gephardt.

Bill leased his land, but he was a hard worker and everyone considered him to be an honest person. Even though I was just 13, he trusted me to do minor tractor evolutions in the different fields.

For example, I was allowed to rake hay for baling. When the baling was completed, I would help gather hay bales from the fields.

In the spring of 1944, I turned 14 and Bill trusted me to drive an old F-20 FarmAll tractor that could pull a plow and prepare or harrow the fields for planting. Of course, this was during World War II when most of the young men, even farmers, were drafted into the armed forces.

As a result, several of us town kids were let out of school early in the afternoons so we could help with the farm work.

I worked for Bill Gephardt until the fall of 1946 when I turned 16.

Chapter 14

Traps, Pelts and Skunks

During most of my high school years, I also operated an animal trap line, mostly for muskrats and mink. Their pelts were very valuable then.

I also set a couple of land traps for an occasional fox.

Early one morning I caught a skunk. I returned to our house to get a shotgun. About that same time, our newspaper delivery boy Bob McCullough happened along. Bob wanted to tag along and see the skunk I had trapped.

Why not, I reasoned, although I did warn him to stay well back until after I had shot the skunk.

I was planning to leave it dead in the trap until evening so I could handle it without getting the smell on me.

However, after I fired the rifle, Bob ran over and picked up the dead skunk. He then left to finish his paper route before heading to school.

I returned the gun, changed clothes, then headed to school. I didn't even get in the school's front door when Principal McCullough, Bob's father, met me at the front door.

As a result of Bob's poor judgment, I received two days suspension from school.

Chapter 15

Earning $1 per Hour

During my junior and senior years of high school, I was also active in basketball and baseball. I lettered in both sports, along with keeping up on all my outside chores.

At age 16, I went to work for another farmer by the name of Joe Gilmore. Joe paid very good wages — $1 per hour — the same wage grown men in light industry were then earning.

Mr. Gilmore lived about two miles from our home, so my uncle Clarence McFate loaned me a horse so I wouldn't have to ride my bicycle or walk.

I continued with farm work until I graduated in 1948 from North Beaver Township High School in New Castle, Penn.

In the fall of 1947, during my senior year, I tried out for a semi-professional football team in a little town three miles from home.

That team was the Wabash Bears, located in Mahoningtown, Penn. I only made the third string, but at least I was on the team.

I played alongside Chuck Tanner, later of Pittsburg Pirates fame. He and I were the only non-Italians on the team.

Just like the sailors on the *Coucal*, the older guys on the football team quickly adopted me.

To them, I could do no wrong.

I played that fall and gained several fine friends.

Even after I graduated high school and enlisted in the Navy, several of them continued to stop by our house to ask my parents how I was doing.

Chapter 16

Baseball with Honus Wagner

In the spring of my senior year of high school, I was invited to Forbes Field — home of the Pittsburgh Pirates — to try out for the professional baseball team. I had received a letter from Honus Wagner, the Baseball Hall of Fame shortstop who played at that time for the Pirates.

I still have his signed letter in my possession today.

Wagner was a friend of my Uncle Will Douglas. What a thrill it was for me to be on the same field with Honus Wagner and to be instructed by one of the greatest ball players of all time.

When my tryout was complete, I overheard Wagner commenting to the team coaches that I would never make it in the major leagues. That assessment stung hard, but I resolved to keep playing and work harder to further develop my baseball skills

In May 1948, I graduated from high school. Since my time with the semi-professional football team had shot down any eligibility hopes I might have had for playing college sports, I decided instead to take a job with American Cyanamid, the same dynamite producing company where my father worked. The job was not to my liking, however.

I traveled to nearby New Castle for a visit with a Navy Recruiter. World War II had just ended and all of the military branches were looking for high school graduates to fill recruiting quotas. They were promising to put people into career-building technical schools through the armed services. These different programs were designed to fill vacancies in the fleet caused by World War II sailors leaving the Navy.

After telling Dad about the many opportunities offered by the Navy, again I asked his opinion.

Having served in the Army during World War I, Dad advised me to enlist in the Navy.

"If you need to eat, the Navy will serve you hot food. If you sleep, the Navy will provide you with a bed," he advised.

Chapter 17

Top to Bottom

I was shaken from my boyhood memories as we approached landfall off Lahaina. This is where the *Coucal* was to anchor for advanced diver training and to exercise our McCann Rescue Chamber, also known as the Diving Bell.

McCann Rescue Chamber

Because the *Coucal*'s primary mission was to serve as a submarine rescue vessel, we had 42 qualified deep divers as part of the ship's company and four qualified diving officers including myself.

Just months before, I had successfully completed the Navy's Deep Diving School in Washington, DC, prior to taking command of the *Coucal*.

At that time, the

primary mission of an Auxiliary Ship Rescue or ASR was to rescue personnel and retrieve sensitive equipment or weapons from a downed submarine to a depth of 1,200 feet. For this reason, we exercised and trained our divers every chance we had.

When I attended the Navy's Deep Diving School, we dove in the murky Anacostia River. The river was so dirty that you could see nothing when you were under water.

Now, however, we were diving in Hawaiian waters and they are clear all the way to the bottom. Anyway, we were anchored just a short boat trip from the town of Lahaina on the island of Maui.

After several other divers had completed their dives, Master Chief Molder Bill Lucree, our ship's master diver, informed me that Navy regulations required that I re-qualify for Deep Diving under his command.

Lucree was well known throughout the diving Navy as the Silver Fox.

I agreed to suit up and then walked — no slim feat while dressed in a diving suit with weights that added 150 pounds to my frame — to the lowering stage, a platform hooked to a boom on the ship. The lowering stage helped a suited diver get over the side and lowered that diver gently down to the bottom, some 110 feet below the keel.

That shouldn't have been a problem for me except that I was afraid of heights.

Well, I was suited up and standing on the stage platform. As they hoisted the stage over the side and started to lower me into the water, I made a serious mistake and looked down.

There was the bottom, some 120 feet below my booted feet!

I immediately took a death grip on the side of the stage and held on for dear life all the way to the ocean's bottom. After a respectable time on the sea floor, they eventually hoisted me back to the surface. However, this time I wisely refused to look down.

For several weeks after the diving exercise, the *Coucal* began a series of Submarine Force Training exercises by supporting some of the Pearl Harbor-based submarines as they conducted their own underway training and diving operations.

Chapter 18

Selected for Command

After successfully requalifying as a Navy Deep Diver, I thought back on the arduous training I received shortly after I was selected to assume command of the *Coucal*.

I had just finished up a stint in Philadelphia training Navy Reserve submariners and I had long dreamed of having my own command at sea.

My 21 years of hard work, first as an enlisted man for 12 years and later as an officer, was finally about to be rewarded.

But before I could assume command of this submarine rescue vessel, I needed to complete the rigorous Navy Deep Diving School in Washington, DC.

This six-month course was necessary to become a qualified deep diving officer.

This piece of news was somewhat challenging as I was 39 years old and classified as a Category 4 or poor swimmer.

I also was in relatively poor physical shape after two years of shore duty with a banged-up knee.

In order to condition my body for the arduous tasks that I knew were ahead of me, I received permission from the Commanding Officer of the Philadelphia Naval Base to use the base pool at my own convenience.

Almost every early morning for four long months, I hit the pool for at least two hours. The swimming helped me greatly in getting my body into somewhat decent physical condition.

I knew that the Navy Deep Diving School would teach me all of the skills of diving far below the surface to accomplish submarine rescue work. While there, I would also learn the rudiments of basic diving medicine that included most of the underwater diving systems used by the Navy at that time.

I also knew this would be a very tough course for someone my age who had grown a bit soft after several years of shore duty. That is what kept me motivated each morning to exercise in the base pool while winding down our family's stay in Philadelphia.

I also spent some time locating a rental house in Woodbridge, Virginia, where my family could reside while I was attending diving school.

Chapter 19

Deep Diving School

I remembered with trepidation the day I finally reported to the Navy Deep Diving School located at the Washington Navy Yard and Navy Gun Factory on the Anacostia River in Washington, DC. Authorized by the first Secretary of the Navy, Benjamin Stoddert, in 1799, this is the US Navy's oldest shore establishment. It occupies land set aside by George Washington for use by the federal government.

The Washington Navy Yard was established in 1799 along the Anacostia River.

During its early years, the Navy Yard became the Navy's largest shipbuilding and ship refitting facility. Twenty-two vessels were constructed on the Yard, ranging from small 70-foot gunboats to the *USS Minnesota*, a 246-foot steam frigate.

In more than two centuries of existence, the Washington Navy Yard has experienced both physical growth and significant changes in mission. Initially established as a storage and shipbuilding facility in the middle of the Nineteenth Century, it was changed to a heavy industrial plant primarily concerned with the development, construction and testing of naval guns.

The facility grew significantly as the Navy expanded during the early 1900s and during the two World Wars, when it produced much of the ordnance material that armed the fleet.

Its name was formally changed to Naval Gun Factory soon after the end of World War II and again to Naval Weapons Plant in 1959 as guided missiles displaced guns as the Navy's principal shipboard armament.

However, within a few years, as part of a general Defense Department shift away from government-owned production facilities, the plant's industrial work ceased and much of its land was diverted to non-navy uses. At this time, its name reverted to Washington Navy Yard.

During the subsequent four decades, it emerged as a major administrative center with a considerable historical presence. More recently, it has seen many of its old industrial buildings modified for new purposes or replaced by modern structures.

Chapter 20

Warmed Over Death

The Anacostia River near the Navy Yard is usually super muddy. The bottom itself is heavily laden with thick layers of silt. Visibility at the surface was only about six inches, and near the bottom was almost zero.

When I arrived at the Navy Deep Diving School and reported in, I was informed that I would follow the same regimen as all of the younger men in regard to my instruction and physical requirements. I was also informed that the instructors, all senior enlisted men, were in charge. Officer trainees were told to leave their ranks at the gate as far as diving instructions went.

True to their word, the next morning upon my arrival at the school, we trainees formed three ranks and did 45 minutes of calisthenics, then a mile-long run. We finished off our physical training session with a 20 minute swim. Only then were we deemed ready to begin our 10-hour training day.

When I arrived at the school, I weighed about 215 pounds. At graduation six months later, I tipped the scales at just 190 pounds.

"You look like warmed-over death," my wife Mary Lou remarked shortly after the graduation ceremony.

I made it through, however. Sadly, some of my training mates did not.

Chapter 21

Protecting
My Candy Ass

Most of my training difficulties came from the heavy helmet that was an integral part of the Navy's deep diving suit at that time.

When it was my turn to go into the water, I put on the canvas suit and then sat on a wooden stool.

One of the other students helped me to get fully dressed.

First came the steel-soled shoes at 45 pounds apiece. Then, my helper set the heavy helmet on my shoulders.

Using wing nuts, he bolted the helmet onto my canvas suit with it's brass collar.

At about this time, I realized fully that the only place I would be able to move very quickly is down to the

A canvas deep dive suit in the 1950s.

bottom of the diving tank, river or ocean.

Since I have very prominent bones on my shoulder blades, each time I put on the diving helmet, the canvas diving suit would rub my shoulders to the point of drawing blood.

As a result, the training unit's doctor devised several felt pads or shims that could be taped onto my shoulders. These were designed to keep the suit and helmet from resting on my raw shoulder blades.

The instructor overseeing each diver's dressing that first day was a crusty Chief Petty Officer with a wicked sense of humor.

About the time the others were getting ready to set the helmet on me, the Chief Petty Officer came over to where I was being suited up.

"Hold it!" he boomed in a very commanding voice.

"We have to put something around Mr. Gibson's ankles," the Chief continued.

I immediately wanted to know what this was all about.

The Chief explained that because of my delicate shoulders, I would need to have kerosene-soaked rags wrapped around my ankles.

Deep sea diving helmet

"Why?" I asked

"To keep the ants away from your candy ass," he bellowed so that everyone could hear.

We all had a good laugh and then I went into the water without any ankle rags.

Chapter 22

Saving the Tree

During our on shore instruction at the Navy Deep Diving School, we learned all about the uses of most types of explosives including plastic explosives. There are many uses for plastic explosives and some of them are unique to that line of work.

One application I remember most vividly included wrapping plastic explosives around the trunk of a tree. When ignited, the explosive cut the tree off as neatly as a chain saw.

However, there was only one tree remaining in the area where we were training.

Of course, we all wanted to see a tree get blown down. But our instructor was the same crusty Chief Petty Officer who had charge of our group during the diving suit dressing exercise. He expressly forbade us to blow the tree down.

"Why?" we all wanted to know.

He told us that a farmer lived near this site and that farmer had a two-legged dog with one front leg and one back leg on the same side of his body. The Chief explained that this dog used the tree to go potty and if we blew the tree down, the dog would have nothing to lean against while raising his hind leg.

Chapter 23

Take Your Bubbles
With You

On another afternoon following a very tough and exhausting day at Deep Diving School, I was wearing my diving suit and on the bottom of the river. But I was really done in physically.

I was supposed to maneuver through the heavy river-bottom silt from one point to another and it was tough going for me with all that heavy diving suit and equipment weighing me down.

Up on the surface, our favorite Chief Petty Officer was directing me by shouting down a long tube attached to my diving helmet.

"Yellow Diver, move out!" he yelled into the communication hose.

"I am moving out," I replied with considerable effort.

However, the soft and very muddy bottom wasn't allowing me to get much of anywhere.

Again from the surface I heard, "Yellow Diver, move out!"

"Damn it! I am moving out!" I shouted back.

"Then take your bubbles with you," the Chief said, nearly choking on his own laughter.

Chapter 24

Managing Buoyancy

During the Deep Diving instructions, there were many very difficult and physically demanding projects that I had to complete.

One of the hardest for me was learning to properly inflate my diving suit to slightly negative buoyancy so I could remain on the bottom yet still be able to maneuver around to complete all of my required projects.

Too much positive buoyancy and I would come to the surface too fast.

During deep dives, that is a serious condition that increases the possibility of getting the bends. To demonstrate this desired state of slightly negative buoyancy, the instructors devised a problem that involved stringing a two-inch line underneath a diving barge floating on the surface.

Once a diver entered the water, he would need to inflate his suit to the proper pressure allowing him to rise enough to grab onto a line extending underneath the barge.

He would then proceed hand over hand from one side of the barge's keel to the other side.

If the diver allowed too much air into his suit, however, the buoyancy would lift him up against the keel of the barge and potentially trap him there.

Too little buoyancy and the suit, boots and helmet would be so heavy that a diver could not hold onto the line. This would send a diver quickly to the silty bottom.

It was a tough problem for me to solve, but I finally mastered the necessary skills.

Finally, to demonstrate how closely divers must work when submerged, our instructors placed a 12-inch by 12-inch timber that was 7 feet long into the murky water.

Using a very large cross-cut saw much like loggers use, two divers on opposite sides of the timber were supposed to saw it in half.

Fully suited, another diver and I were loaded into the water carrying the saw. We were inter-connected with talker headsets. In order to cut the timber in two, we needed to coordinate our pulls and pushes on the saw handles while maintaining contact between the saw's blade and the wooden timber.

By far, this was the most demanding physical project we were assigned to complete.

When they brought our project back up to the surface, we had indeed sawed the timber in two pieces.

However, instead of cutting it perpendicularly straight across, we had cut it on a 45-degree angle, thus requiring much more physical effort. As a result of my exertion, the inside of my diving suit was soaked with sweat.

After reliving those memories, I was once again thrust into the realities of my new command responsibilities on board the *Coucal*.

Chapter 25

Walking on Eggshells

Finally, the *Coucal* was ordered to report to the Commander Pacific Fleet Training Group for a very intense two-week training period.

Surface ships are required to go through this type of training every so often to ensure that the ship and its crew are performing as required. This was also a great work up for the ship's upcoming WestPac deployment.

We were now placed under Commander Fleet Training Group's operational control and guidance for the entire two-week period. During the training exercise, the entire crew was instructed on the proper operation of a surface ship while at sea.

The Pacific Fleet Training Group is staffed with very senior enlisted personnel and several very sharp ex-enlisted officers. They were all experts in their respective fields. The ship was examined thoroughly and the crew was trained both for in-port and underway operations.

This type of shipboard training was and is very serious. Results of the training are reported all the way up the chain of command to the Fleet Commander.

It was my intention to have my ship properly trained and examined. I therefore informed both our crew and the Fleet

Training Group that the *Coucal* would cooperate in each and every way possible or I was to be informed.

From personal observations and the random scuttlebutt that I overheard, I was aware that the *Coucal* suffered from a very serious lack of training during the past several years. For many reasons, there was also a very serious on-board morale problem.

The officers were overly cautious.

They were afraid to make serious decisions for fear of being second-guessed and badgered by the previous skipper. The Chief Petty Officers were under-informed and unsure of their own positions, let alone the responsibilities and functions of those sailors under their command.

To counter these problems, Executive Officer Ben Benites and I held several wardroom meetings with our junior officers as well as the Chief Petty Officers in attendance where we assured them that they should step forward and take charge of every situation.

If they did so, the Executive Officer and I would back them fully. However, if they made a mistake, they would hear about it directly.

From then on, we had a very strong Chief's Quarters. Most of the officers stepped up to the challenge and did their jobs in a very professional manner.

This was an intense time of personal adjustment and learning, as well as overseeing those shifts in thinking that I was requiring of the junior officers and enlisted sailors under my command.

I was reminded of a similar period on board the *USS Catfish* when I joined an entire wardroom of new officers tasked with turning that submarine and its crew around.

Chapter 26

Averting Disaster

After arriving in San Diego and getting my family settled into our home there, I reported to the *USS Catfish*, which was visiting in Vancouver, British Columbia. The *Catfish* was on a shake-down cruise following an extended shipyard period.

The skipper, Commander James Varley, was a fine officer. The Executive Officer was Lieutenant Commander James Patton, one of the finest Navy officers for whom I have ever served. Not only was Jim Patton very intelligent, he also had a set of standards that few Navy officers could reach, let alone maintain. He always required maximum performance from each of his officers.

At the time of my reporting for duty, however, the *Catfish* had a less than sterling reputation.

She had also failed a recent administrative inspection.

The officers then on board were being transferred one by one. As a result, Captain Varley, Executive Officer Patton and three other officers including myself all reported on board in a very short period of time. This stepped-up officer rotation was done intentionally to help bring this submarine's crew up to normal submarine performance standards.

I was to be the new Weapon's Officer, also known informally as Gun Boss. As I was the newest officer onboard, I also had the honor of being the Officer of the Deck on the day we were to get underway.

Upon leaving port, I was relieved as Officer of the Deck so I went below. I stopped briefly by the officer's wardroom for a drink of water, then stepped into the forward Torpedo Room.

I could scarcely believe what my eyes were witnessing. The men were moving a torpedo towards an open firing tube without any restraining lines or handling gear attached to the tube-like projectile. To make matters worse, the Mark 14 torpedo they were handling weighed more than 2,000 pounds.

For practical purposes, the torpedo was loose while the submarine was underway and entering the open sea. Any unforeseen wave action or radical maneuvering could have been catastrophic.

I immediately called attention to this dangerous situation and ordered a tie down strap to be applied over the torpedo, thus fastening it securely to the loading skid on which the torpedo was resting.

Once it was secured, I ordered the men to wait until they had the proper equipment to safely place the torpedo into the assigned firing tube. On orders of the Executive Officer, I also immediately relieved the present Weapons Officer of his duties.

Chapter 27

Mary Lou to the Rescue

"They also serve who only stand and wait."
Mrs. Eleanor Rickover
Ship's sponsor at the launching
of the *USS Hyman G. Rickover*

I now set about reestablishing the boat's Weapons Department so that the ship could once again be proud of it and so that the department would function safely and properly.

Thanks to a fine group of dedicated enlisted men and a very knowledgeable Chief Petty Officer, the Weapons Department started to take shape. With a considerable amount of elbow grease, the torpedo rooms also started looking almost brand new.

While topside, a deck force consisting of several non-rated men led by a petty officer worked overtime chipping and painting the entire superstructure so *Catfish* would once again be presentable to anyone visiting.

When finished, the topside area would be properly preserved with paint and lacquer for our times at sea. It would also be better able to withstand the harshness of salt water and wave action while underway, whether on the surface or submerged.

We then rewrote and installed a new operations manual for the weapons department.

In due time, all department personnel had written orders for every step while performing their duties.

My wife Mary Lou was once again a great help to me in typing up this vast amount of paper work on an old manual typewriter because the ship's yeoman was way too busy with other duties.

Mary Lou did this work for me in addition to raising our two boys and making a very pleasant home for all of us.

Chapter 28

Sinking a Destroyer

"When you shoot at a destroyer and miss,
it's like hitting a wildcat in the ass with a banjo."
Steward Dogan
Chief Petty Officer
USS Gurnard during World War II

During this time, the *USS Catfish* was required to conduct a very serious at-sea weapons test.

This was for advanced weapons training and to show that the *Catfish*'s weapons department was once again back up to acceptable performance standards.

For this test, the boat was ordered to load several Mark 14 World War II-type steam-driven torpedoes with explosive war heads installed and make them ready for firing. Before loading, we also had to prepare and check out these steam-driven torpedoes to make sure they were in good working order.

Once we completed that assignment, the *Catfish* was ordered out to sea so that we could fire two of those torpedoes at an unmanned, remote-controlled World War II-era destroyer that had been mothballed for just such a purpose. Our goal was to sink that ship.

After arriving on station and submerging our boat, we immediately went to Battle Stations, Torpedo Status.

The Captain and the fire control party worked the submarine into a correct firing solution.

When all was ready and there was a correct fire control solution, we let loose those two torpedoes. Then, the entire crew waited with hardly a sound for a report from our sonar operator that the torpedoes were running "hot, straight, and normal."

Until we had that report, the entire crew worried that one or both of those torpedoes might circle back to hit our own submarine.

Well, the torpedoes did run true on the very course the fire control party had set. They hit the destroyer right in the middle of target (MOT), splitting the heavily armored ship in half.

With such a massive hit of explosive power, the targeted destroyer sank almost immediately.

In true World War II submarine fashion, we returned to port with a broom attached to the number one periscope indicating a clean sweep. This was tradition that we adopted to help raise morale on our boat.

I've never been so relieved that the ship's Weapons Department was finally up to snuff and able to pull off this operational test without a glitch. Now, I thought to myself, I can ease up on the guys some.

Well, that was not to be the case.

Chapter 29

Working Nights and Weekends

The very next day, Executive Officer Lieutenant Commander Patton told me to relieve the Engineering Officer. But first he had to relieve me as Gun Boss so that I could now more freely work with the Engineering Department. All of this was done just prior to a very serious administrative inspection to be conducted by the Division Commander in six short weeks.

At the same time, our boat was also preparing for a six-month WestPac deployment cruise. This meant there would be many more nights spent aboard, as well as weekends spent with members of the boat's Engineering Department as we completely reworked and rewrote that department's standard instructions and operating procedures manual.

These instructions laid out the proper way the Engineering Department was to operate and maintain all of the various systems within that department.

Once again, I relied heavily on Mary Lou's typing skills to rescue me from that arduous task.

Throughout this period, the *Catfish* was conducting daily operations off the coast near San Diego in order to train our entire crew on proper underway procedures. Mary Lou very readily came to our rescue and typed up those instructions as well.

Chapter 30

Blood, Sweat and Tears

The *USS Catfish*'s 10 officers and 71 enlisted crew members now stood for the forthcoming administrative inspection — a grueling two days — until the boat was given an outstanding grade in all departments. This was a complete turnaround in the submarine's performance, a testimony to the boat's strong leadership on all levels.

With motivated officers, it is amazing what such a large team can do in a very short time.

Later that same year, the boat was awarded the coveted Battle Efficiency E award.

The *Catfish* and its crew had come a long way, thanks in great part to the leadership of Captain Varley and the entire wardroom, led by Lieutenant Commander Patton and a fine group of dedicated and hard-working officers and the men they led. As someone once said, "This was only accomplished through blood, sweat and tears."

Finally, we were pronounced ready to load out the submarine and head to WestPac for our six-month duty tour.

Chapter 31

Fast Cruising

Remembering how Captain Varley, Lieutenant Commander Patton and all of the wardroom officers on the *USS Catfish* had managed that submarine's total reversal in morale gave me renewed confidence for the daunting task of accomplishing something similar on the *Coucal*.

USS Catfish (SS 339) underway   US Navy photo

I was confident that with the help of my Executive Officer Ben Benites and our entire wardroom staff, the crew of the *Coucal* could, through hard work and persistence, make the same 180-degree turnaround in attitude as well as enthusiasm.

With just days to go before the *Coucal* was scheduled to leave port, I decided to borrow a procedure picked up while serving on the Atlantic Coast with nuclear powered submarines.

During my time in Submarine Squadron Eighteen, I observed that they used a Fast Cruise or pre-underway system of checking all of the mechanical systems as well as the stationing of crew members to make sure that everyone knew their various assignments prior to actually getting underway.

To my knowledge, this Fast Cruise procedure had never been used on a surface ship until I tried it on the *Coucal*.

So before we left port, the officers and I devised a special sea and anchor detail that went through every space on the ship just as if we were actually getting underway.

This was Fast Cruise testing while still tied to the pier, moored alongside a tender or, in some cases, even while at anchor.

Either the day before or early the same day that we were actually going to get underway, the crew would stand to their underway maneuvering stations and operate each item or system. This evolution not only exercised the ship's systems, but also helped us to find out whether we were short of trained personnel in any critical area.

This was a new procedure to the crew of the *Coucal*, a surface ship, and it did raise some eyebrows. But time and again, by using this procedure before actually getting underway, we were able to find and correct problems that might have caused serious problems had we actually been in the process of leaving a port.

Chapter 32

Engineman School

I soon realized that just as I had been trained as a raw recruit, I and the other officers needed to retrain our entire crew in some of the rudimentary steps of their duties and responsibilities aboard the *Coucal*.

This realization took me back to my own beginnings as a Navy recruit.

I had enlisted right out of high school on what was called a minority cruise of three years duration. I signed up for the Navy's Engineman School where I would be trained as a diesel mechanic once I had successfully completed my basic recruit training.

As July 7, 1948, came around, I headed off to Pittsburgh for physicals and a swearing in ceremony for the US Navy. All the new recruits then boarded a train — my first such ride — bound for Waukegan, Illinois, and the Great Lakes Naval Training Center.

Oh what a change of environment that was!

We arrived at 0200 or 2 a.m. We stepped off the train and right away people started yelling at me, a poor naive boy from Mount Jackson, Pennsylvania.

This really shook me up.

Not even my coaches had ever yelled at me like that. I was especially concerned when the drill instructor informed me that I was not too bright and that my parents were never married.

My group of 120 recruits entered a world that was entirely new to each of us.

We were informed that this group of young men would be our boot camp company. We were issued Navy uniforms and given a canvas duffel or sea bag in which to store our spare uniform items. We then packed up our civilian clothes and sent them home.

The medical corpsmen administered each of us the required shots. Most of us didn't feel very good for a couple of days. In Navy jargon, we had what was commonly called "cat fever."

After those ordeals, a sailor in charge shared his opinion that it was a waste of government funds, but the Navy was going to feed us breakfast anyway.

My first meal in the Navy consisted of creamed hard boiled eggs on toast.

Because of "cat fever" I was not feeling the joy of food at all.

I took one look at the mess on my steel tray and that ended any desire I might have had to consume my first Navy meal.

Chapter 33

Climbing a Fence

After successfully enduring 12 weeks of harassment, I graduated from Navy boot camp.

At that time, even I realized that this former raw recruit was more grown up than the high school graduate who had arrived just 12 weeks previous.

Another thing that surprised me about that experience was when I finally realized that the Chief Petty Officers, our drill instructors, were actually human beings who could speak in a normal tone of voice.

This realization triggered a pleasant memory of a humorous experience.

Our Company Commander, Chief McKee, was assigned Chief Feldman as an assistant. Feldman was very new, however, to the training of recruits. This was made fully evident while we were up on the drill field, better known to us as the grinder, where we were doing some close-order marching drills.

Based on Chief Feldman's most recent command, our platoon was heading directly toward a perimeter fence. As we got ever closer to the barrier, the Chief grew flustered and even more confused.

As the first members of our platoon came into contact with the obstacle, we did what any group of young men would do. We started to climb over.

Finally, the Chief came up with an unusual command.

"Come away from that fence! COME!" he barked.

Once our recruit training was complete, it was again time to cross the grinder drill field. However, this time it was to attend Class A in Engineman School.

Chapter 34

Fireman Apprentice

It was late fall by this time, and growing colder ever day as we approached winter at the Great Lakes Naval Training Center along Lake Michigan.

I studied small diesel engines for 12 weeks, but I also was recruited to play quarterback for the Engineman School's football team in the Great Lakes Intramural League.

It was very cold playing sports outdoors, but we had a lot of fun.

When Engineman School ended, I was promoted from Fireman Recruit E-1 to Fireman Apprentice E-2. It wasn't much of a promotion as far as rank and responsibility went, but it did mean I received a pay raise of $12 a month.

I was also very fortunate to be allowed to travel home on leave for Christmas in 1948.

When I came back to Great Lakes, I received orders to report to New London, Conn., for eight weeks of submarine school.

To this day, I do not remember ever actually volunteering for submarine school. But the only way you could get into submarine school was to volunteer, so somewhere along the way I must have signed my name on the bottom line.

Chapter 35

Submarine School

When I arrived in New London, the area was still in the firm grips of winter.

All newly arrived students were given the privilege of shoveling the falling snow for a week and a half. And there was quite a lot of snow building up as those cold, wet clouds blew over the lake.

Our first contact at this eight-week submarine school was a lecture on the pitfalls of a New London liberty. The Chief Petty Officer in charge was very salty and did everything by-the-book.

He was also demanding and required all students to toe the line. He stood in front of us and informed us all that although there were 120 of us lowly peons in this upcoming class, only 60 of us would actually graduate.

The school officials and instructors would use any excuse to drop students, he warned.

A shipmate of mine, Len Glendening, and I took those threats seriously. We never once left the base for the entire eight weeks of submarine school.

We were too afraid of running afoul of the shore patrol. Any infraction, no matter how minor, would mean we could be dropped from the submarine school training program.

Chapter 36

Momsen's Lung

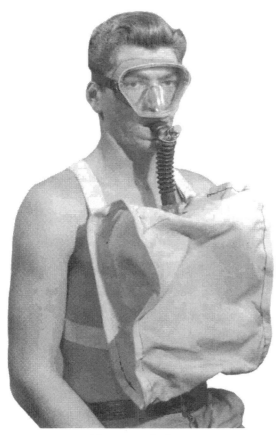

Momsen's Lung

It was at about this same time in our basic training that we were introduced to the Momsen Lung. This was a device used to escape from a downed submarine.

The Momsen Lung was an apparatus that acted as an outside-the-body air chamber so we could breathe while under water. It also allowed a diver to get rid of the excess pressure building up in the lungs while safely returning to the surface.

To simulate deep water, the Navy had constructed two very large cylindrical water tanks that stood 120 foot high. These were used to train students in the use of the Momsen lung and proper escape procedures.

One of those two tanks was located at the submarine base in Groton, Connecticut, while the other was at the Navy's submarine base in Pearl Harbor, Hawaii.

The Momsen Lung system was used for several more years following our training, but was eventually replaced by more modern escape procedures as time went by.

Chapter 37

First Submarine Ride

This also was when I received my first ride on a Navy ship and my first look at an actual submarine.

My class was taken to sea to indoctrinate us and show us what it was like on an active submersible boat. We got underway on a very famous World War II submarine, the *USS Flyingfish* (SS-229). After getting out to sea, it was time to dive under the waves.

As a student, my duty station was in the pump room, a small compartment located underneath the submarine's Control Room.

It is also where they release air when venting negative tank. This happens when the submarine has reached its assigned depth and must then level off.

The venting of this tank is very routine and is a part of every diving procedure. But no one told me that a lot of air, salt spray and loud noise would come shooting out of a pipe positioned right by my feet.

To be honest, the venting scared the hell out of me.

For a few moments, I wasn't sure whether submarine duty was really a career for me.

Chapter 38

Dirty Laundry; Dirty Tricks

After Submarine school, I was ordered to the *USS Conger* (SS-477) home ported on the western coast of Panama. Before I could join the *Conger*, however, there was a two-week stay at the Norfolk, Virginia, Naval Base, a personnel receiving station and shipping-out point.

That was where I learned the art of washing dishes in the base galley. That assignment had me cleaning dishes and metal serving trays for the entire Navy base.

It was with some relief when I finally boarded the *USS Adams* (APA–19) for transport to Panama. Our passage included two weeks of rough water, the worst of which we encountered while sailing around Cape Hatteras, located off the coast of North Carolina.

That part of the Atlantic Ocean is almost always very rough.

As a side note, the old salts on board any ship always like to play tricks on new recruits.

My work space and my watch station were in the forward engine room. Because of the work I was doing, my work pants or dungarees quickly became very dirty.

The most senior Chief Petty Officer, being very helpful, ordered me up to the fantail at the stern of the ship and told me to ask one of the boatswain mates who worked there for permission to tie my dirty dungarees to a small rope so I could trail them behind the ship to get them clean.

The boatswain mates were more than eager to help teach this raw recruit a lesson.

Once my dungarees were in the sea, I was told to return the following day and the boatswain mates would help me retrieve my clothes. As directed, the next day I went back to the fantail and, true to their word, the sailors there retrieved the tattered remains of my dungarees.

Only about six inches of rags remained on the line. The combination of salty water and turbulence from the ship's propeller had done short work to eat the cloth away. So much for an old salt's education of a new recruit.

Chapter 39

Time for Fishing

Time and again during my early training as well as throughout my career, I experienced firsthand how humor and recreation can improve the morale of even the most bitter and jaded seaman. At other times, I found solace and renewal in fishing and hunting at various duty stations or while attending a specialized training program.

There were several other things that the officers and I devised to make the *Coucal* a hard-working vessel, but also a happier and more pleasurable place in which to work and live while we were all on board.

As an avid fisherman, I knew that there was a certain species of fish that roamed the Pacific Ocean around Hawaii. This fish is called Mahi-Mahi, but is better known to some as dolphins. They are very large fish that are fun to catch and even better to eat.

Coucal's most economical cruising speed was 9 knots or about 10.5 miles per hour. Would you believe that is also the correct speed for trolling Mahi-Mahi and Ahi (tuna).

Well, our ship borrowed the proper fishing gear from the Submarine Base's recreation department and, when safe to do so, we cruised with two outrigger fishing poles and one pole mounted at the center of our fantail.

Whenever a fish was hooked, the bridge would be notified and, if safe, the ship would come to a full stop.

Most times, the hooked fish was successfully hauled aboard. We caught 69 Mahi-Mahi and many pounds of Ahi (tuna) as well as one marlin off the coast of Saipan during the 17 months I had command of the *Coucal*.

During our first WestPac tour, we donated a couple hundred pounds of fish to a children's orphanage when we arrived in Yokosuka, Japan.

Chapter 40

Boosting Morale

Most days, however, the *Coucal* was a very hard-working ship with lots of deck rigging to accomplish. This was especially true when we would train for our specialty, the rescue of a downed submarine and its crew.

When engaged in this type of work, we would put the ship into a four-point moor, one anchor on each point of a large rectangle with our boat moored at its center.

This evolution required the use of four anchors housed on the fantail. Heavy chain had to be wrestled out and laid down or draped over the port and starboard sides of the ship along the after deck.

That was hard, dirty labor.

Whenever this evolution was going on, there was always a pot of soup and a plate of sandwiches close by in the ship's galley.

Also, even though it was against Navy regulations, I authorized one beer per sailor every Sunday afternoon while we were underway. Our sailors worked very hard almost all the time and this gave them a small reward for their loyalty and efforts.

Deck work is not only very dirty, it is very difficult to stand on a heaving deck in high seas and through all sorts of weather.

Therefore, I directed our supply officer, Warrant Officer Jimmy Gee, now retired as a Lieutenant Commander, to go to the salvage area on the main Pearl Harbor Submarine Base and procure as many pairs of old US Marine Corps fatigues for use as work uniforms.

This would allow our deck hands to wear their rugged Marine Corps fatigues during our four point mooring operations so that they did not ruin their good Navy dungarees.

Chapter 41

Paybacks are Hell!

We also allowed fun things to happen on board the *USS Coucal*.

Practical jokes were allowed as long as they didn't hurt anyone. Nor did we allow them to get personal. In fact, several of these pranks even happened to me.

Early one morning, I was on the ship's bridge and sitting in the captain's chair when one of the lookouts reported seeing something unusual on the horizon. I reached over to pick up my binoculars and quickly took a look in the direction he pointed. Seeing nothing, however, I soon put down my binoculars to get a wider view of what the lookout was apparently referring to.

Again, seeing nothing, I placed my binoculars back in their case. That is when the bridge crew erupted in laughter.

Being the butt of a joke, I did not understand the point of their laughter that continued even as I left the bridge and returned to my cabin. However, when I arrived there and finally looked into the mirror, staring back at me was a giant raccoon with black circles around each eye.

Someone had apparently placed black shoe polish on the rubberized eye shields of my binoculars. It was a great joke on me.

As on any ship or submarine, however, the joke couldn't stay secret even one minute.

I later found out the culprit was a very fine electrician's mate.

It did take me a couple of months, but I eventually returned the favor and got even in a very funny way.

Somehow, this same sailor ended up with a raw egg in the toe of each of his boots. Assisted by our Chief Boatswain Mate, I had placed the raw eggs there very carefully while the unsuspecting sailor was asleep.

As they say, "Paybacks are Hell!"

Chapter 42

Personal Touch

During my 17 months aboard the *USS Coucal*, I fully enjoyed being its Commanding Officer.

Fortunately for me, I learned early on that a Captain can be too omnipresent. Once trained up to my demanding standards, I also knew the officers and crew needed to be trusted to perform their duties without worrying that the Captain might be spying on them.

As a result, I spent a lot of time in my cabin writing personal letters to the wives and family members of the crew.

Unknown to me until I started writing this book, my wife Mary Lou found some of these mimeographed epistles and presented them to me. One such message written Oct. 31, 1970, was mailed from the Fleet Post Office in San Francisco.

> Dear Mary Lou,
>
> As we depart Yokosuka, Japan, I wanted to take a moment to update all the families and loved ones of COUCAL personnel. We departed Pearl Harbor, Hawaii, on 10 September and after a smooth trip arrived in Guam, Marianas Islands, on the 24th of September.

En-route to Guam, we crossed the 180th Meridian (the International Date Line) and conducted a brief ceremony to initiate the new men into the realms of the "Golden Dragon."

The ship stopped on the 180th and we had the men being initiated swim across the imaginary line. As they crossed the line, they also swam from Monday to Tuesday, taking about five minutes.

During our stay in Guam, while under the operational control of the Commander of Naval Forces, Marianas, we did some very important work for the US government in and around Guam.

COUCAL personnel performed magnificently as claimed in the following messages:

> FROM COMMANDER NAVAL
> FORCES, MARIANAS:
>
> Upon your departure from Guam, I would like to take this opportunity to commend the officers and men of COUCAL for a job well done.
>
> The enthusiasm and professionalism displayed by you in executing your mission was most satisfying.
>
> It has been a sincere pleasure having you serve in my command.

May smooth seas and following winds prevail for the remainder of your deployment.

Signed: *Admiral Pugh*

FROM COMMANDER,
ANTISUBMARINE WARFARE
FORCES, PACIFIC:

At the completion of operations that you were tasked with, I note with pleasure the fine professional performances of the officers and men of the COUCAL.

Your efforts have added significantly to our detailed knowledge of the strategic Philippine Sea/Mariana Basin and have provided another example of Navy team work.

I extend my personal appreciation.

Signed: *Admiral Aurand*

We departed Guam and headed for Yokosuka, Japan, with a six-hour stopover in ChiChi Jima in the Bonin Islands.

Even though the stopover was brief, we still managed to play the Japanese a softball game. They defeated us 5 to 3.

All hands thoroughly enjoyed themselves. Throughout our trip thus far, the sailing has been smooth and the ship has performed superbly, both mechanically and personnel-wise.

All this is the direct result of the hard work
done by all of the crew.

Sincerely,

Jim

J. W. Gibson
Lieutenant Commander, U.S. Navy
Commanding Officer

Whenever I would get too bored in my own stateroom, I would
wander down to the officers wardroom and bother the galley
stewards. Sometimes I would help them make a salad or get even
more involved and cook something special for lunch.

One day, I caught one of our fine young officers, Lieutenant Junior
Grade Peter Fawcett, now a retired Commander, peeking around a
corner.

"Pete, what are you doing down here?" I asked him.

"Captain, I am seeing what I have to like for lunch!" Pete retorted
with a grin.

I also used some of my stateroom time to complete several college
correspondence courses from Pennsylvania State University.

These courses all had to do with agriculture and farming,
something I hoped to use when I eventually retired from the US
Navy.

Chapter 43

Transversing the Isthmus

With some of my free time, I remembered fondly my first days as a young sailor after basic training and Engineman School.

My thoughts traveled swiftly back to those heady days as an 18-year-old Engineman en route to his first ship assignment. Once again I was mentally heading toward my assignment to the *USS Conger*.

After two weeks of passage , we finally arrived in Coco Solo, Panama, on the eastern side of the Panama Canal. Several of us were going by land across the Isthmus of Panama to Balboa and the Rodman Naval Base where my future home, the *USS Conger*, was moored.

We boarded a small train that everyone called the Toonerville Trolley and proceeded to transit the Panamanian rain forest or jungle in route to Balboa and my first submarine duty.

That jungle ride was the first time I had ever seen a live monkey in the wild or caught sight of bananas hanging in large clusters from a tree-like banana plant.

For the most part, our train ride took us alongside the Panama Canal.

This was not such a bad adventure for a kid straight out of Mount Jackson, Penn., a town of about 250 people.

Many years later, my wife and I transited the Panama Canal, but this time we were sailing aboard a passenger cruise ship.

What a difference a few years make.

Balboa is now a very large city with a sky-line that reminds me of San Diego, California.

Chapter 44

Hot Bunking on the *Conger*

Finally, I reported on board the *USS Conger* (SS-477). The *Conger* and six other submarines, along with the submarine tender *Orion* (AS-18), comprised Submarine Squadron Six.

At the end of World War II, there were too many submarines based in Pearl Harbor. That was when Squadron Six was repositioned to Panama.

The *Conger*, commissioned in early 1945, was one of the squadron's newer submarines. For that day and age, it was very shipshape and modern.

After going below decks, I reported to the Chief of the Boat. He was the senior enlisted man on board. He informed me that the *Conger* was over-crowded and thus I would have to hot bunk with two other men.

Hot bunking is where three men use two bunks. Since one of the three men is always on watch duty, the other two can use the two assigned bunks to relax or sleep. When the man on watch comes off duty, one of the other two men in the bunks would go on duty.

This way, the two bunks were always in use or hot.

I was also informed that since there were no lockers available, I would have to live out of my sea bag for a few weeks until there was a spare locker for me to use.

My first duty assignment was as a mess cook. That is an enlisted waiter for the Crew's Mess or enlisted men's dining room. We mess cooks did all the things that guys in the Army do in what they call KP or Kitchen Patrol. We peeled potatoes, washed dishes and made salad when there were fresh vegetables on board.

When submarines leave port on patrol or extended operations, there is a loading plan for everything that has to come on board. Food items are stored throughout the submarine in various locations. There were two such storage spaces below the Crew's Mess. Down there also was a walk-in freezer where meats and other frozen items were stored.

Alongside the freezer was a cool box where eggs, milk and fresh vegetables were kept.

The remaining food was stored throughout the boat. For instance, coffee in five gallon cans was placed in the engine room, outboard of the main engines. Potatoes were stored in the torpedo rooms. Cases of canned goods would be spread out on the decks of different compartments with sheets of plywood placed over them so crew members could safely walk over that area.

Fresh vegetables would last aboard ship only about three weeks. The last to go bad, other than potatoes, were the cabbages and raw carrots. Potatoes would last about six weeks.

Milk and eggs lasted about the same length of time if stored in the refrigeration units.

Meals were planned around this schedule, so if we stayed out to sea more than six or eight weeks, our food came from tin cans. My mess cook duty lasted about two months.

Chapter 45

Getting Qualified

During this time of training on the *Conger*, I was required to work on our submarine qualifications as were all the other newbies. This involved knowing and understanding the workings of the entire submarine and all of its systems.

The idea behind this program was to insure that if a casualty happened and I was alone in any area of the boat, then I could secure that area until help arrived.

To aid my memory, I obtained a notebook in which I made drawings of the hydraulic, air and fuel systems as well as the electrical circuits. Once I had them all on paper, I would be tested orally and my drawings reviewed and signed off by a qualified person.

This training went along with the usual duties of a ten-hour day. I mess-cooked with another newcomer, Ray McCool, a very fine fellow from New Hampshire.

After my tour as a mess cook, I was assigned to the deck force. There, we had lots of different duties. When in port, the deck force worked on the topside areas chipping paint and repainting areas exposed to salt water whenever we were at sea.

We also stood topside security watches when in port. These duties were rotated, so every three days, one of us could count on having the duty assignment to stand watch.

When underway and on the surface, we stood lookout watches on the conning tower bridge.

We stood alongside the Officer of the Deck (OOD) and served as the eyes and ears of the boat. In other words, we reported everything we saw or heard to the OOD.

I would quickly learn that this was wonderful duty while sailing in the tropics, but a bitterly cold job in the North Atlantic, especially during the winter months while patrolling around the Arctic Circle.

When the boat was about to dive, we would hear the OOD shout, "Clear the Bridge!"

That was our signal to scramble through the conning tower's upper hatch and climb down a narrow metal ladder into the control room.

Meanwhile, a loud klaxon alarm would be sounding and the OOD would shout, "Dive! Dive!" into the 1MC, a general announcing system that was wired to loudspeakers mounted throughout the boat.

Once in the Control Room, it was the watchman's duty to turn one of two very large wheels that controlled the diving planes.

Through an intricate hydraulic system, these wheels operated the bow and stern planes or fins that controlled the depth and angle of the submarine's travel through the water when submerged.

On the *USS Conger*, I stood those watches for some time.

Chapter 46

Non-Combatant

When I joined the *Conger*, most of the other crew members had served on submarines during World War II. Each of them had completed many war patrols against the Japanese Navy.

When and if the submarines they served on had completed a mission to sink ships or whatever duties they had been assigned, it was called a successful war patrol. The crew members aboard at that time were then authorized to wear a submarine combat pin on their uniforms, along with any of their other medals and appropriate ribbons.

Of course, those who came on board after World War II were not authorized to wear those pins.

In addition, I and several others who came aboard with me were not yet qualified in submarines. For these shortcomings, the other crew members constantly chided us as "non-quals."

In fact, until I was qualified I thought my name was "You unqualified non-combatant SOB!" Remember, this was in the old Navy where an individual's feelings were not paramount.

As a further part of our training and indoctrination, whenever we did something wrong we were woefully reminded of it and often.

Chapter 47

Engineman Duties

*"Some ships are designed to sink . . .
others require our assistance."*
T-shirt slogan worn by crew
USS Montpelier (SSN-765)

Our Commanding Officer on the *USS Conger* was Davis Cone. He
was a very large man, about six-feet, four-inches tall. He has
appeared in some of the World War II submarine films as the
officer who is using the periscope with an old style green baseball
cap on his head and the stub of a cigar protruding from his lips.

Davis Cone was the former torpedo and gunnery officer on the
USS Bowfin (SS-287) during World War II where he earned the
Navy's Silver Star award. He was a very demanding Commanding
Officer who fully understood the capabilities and limitations of the
submarine he now commanded.

Since I was being trained as an Engineman, I was ordered to go to
the forward Engine Room and report to Howard "Stinky" Davis,
then the Petty Officer in charge.

The Commanding Officer told me that since the boat's engines
were my training specialty, they were now my responsibility no
matter how little I knew about 1,600 horsepower Fairbanks and
Morse engines.

Since the boat was overstaffed with enlisted men, I went back to the engine room and reported to Engineman First Class Davis.

His words of greeting still ring in my ears.

"I don't need you or want you. The first screw up, you're out of here," Davis admonished me.

I was what was called an oiler. It was my job to keep things picked up and to wipe down any and all oil spills. I also had to take notes and make a record of the engine's functions from different gauges once each hour.

The oiler also had responsibility for going to the mess hall to get coffee for the throttle man standing watch because throttle men were not allowed to leave the engine room.

Chapter 48

Learning a Lesson

It was under Stinky Davis that I first learned the submariner's creed: "You are only as good as your word."

One morning while still in port, I was working in the lower flats or bilges, way down below the engines. I had done a really good job of cleaning, I thought, except for one little area in the after-end of the space.

Engineman Davis called down and told me to come up for lunch.

When I came up, he asked me whether I was finished with my cleaning job.

"I am," I replied, thinking that after my lunch I would quickly go back to finish cleaning up that one small area that I had missed.

"Go have lunch," he said.

After lunch I returned to the engine room and went back down to the bilges to pick up the little pile of trash that I knew I had left behind.

During my absence, however, it seemed that every trash can on the entire boat had been dumped in that area.

I knew better than to say anything to anyone. After several more hours and lots of sweat, the lower flats were finally spotless.

When I came up, Engineman Davis was waiting for me.

I will clean up his comments for publication, but what he basically said was, "If you ever lie to me again, I will knock you on your ass."

I have never forgotten that lesson.

Chapter 49

Humor in Uniform

There are several funny stories connected with my time on *USS Conger*.

When ported in Panama, those who had liberty would get away from the area around the submarine mooring pier at Rodman Naval Base.

Outside the base, there was a small town perched up in the hills where we would go on liberty. It was a very cheap way to spend the weekend as there were several bars with stag shows.

Believe me, there is more flesh shown on television today than we ever saw in those stag shows. Down there, *cerveza* (Spanish for beer) was 10 cents a bottle. Rum and Coca-Cola was 15 cents a drink — a nickel for the rum and a dime for the Coke.

Engineman Howard "Stinky" Davis had access to a 1934 sedan whenever we were in port, so he would drive a group of us to the hillside village. The car had a faulty carburetor, however, so one of us would be required to ride on a fender and pour gasoline into the engine to keep it running.

The pourer was an important position because he could stop pouring whenever he desired a pit stop or a bit of fun.

Of course, the rest of us were using Rum and Coke for our own personal fuel.

Engineman Davis was my boss and, in most cases, I followed his directions very carefully.

One day while we were still in port, he informed me that he was going up on the base and was going to get a hair-cut. He suggested I should get one as well.

I received my haircut first. It cost me 15 cents. Then I waited for Davis to finish.

As I waited, I noticed that in one of the other chairs sat a Lieutenant who was also getting his hair cut.

The barbers for Davis and the Lieutenant each finished at about the same time. As was the custom down there, the barbers always sprinkled bay rum, a very fragrant tonic, on your head and gave you a little scalp massage to finish out their service.

The barber was about to put some tonic on the Lieutenant's head until the Lieutenant put up a hand to stop him.

"None of that smelly stuff on me," the Lieutenant declared.

"My wife will think I've been in a French whorehouse."

Whereupon, Davis spoke up.

"Put lots on me!" Davis exclaimed.

"My wife has never been in a French whorehouse."

Chapter 50

Another Lesson Learned

While I was still in Submarine School, one lesson was drilled into us time and again.

When reporting on board a submarine, immediately check the Watch, Quarter and Station billeting posted in the After Battery Compartment or Mess Hall. The list denotes where you stand to perform your underway watch duties. It also shows when and where you are to sleep.

Further, it lets you know where you are to report for battle stations.

One evening after a liberty leave, we were informed that the next morning we would be getting underway for at-sea training. This meant the boat would be taking lots of dives and it also meant we would be at battle stations.

I immediately went to the After Battery Compartment and checked the Watch, Quarter and Station billet. There was my name, as big as life. It stated that I was to go to the engine room on the announcement of Battle Stations, Torpedo.

When I looked for Battle Station, Gun Action, the billet indicated I was to be the "hot shell" man on deck.

The *USS Conger* carried a large, 5-inch, 25-caliber cannon topside on the afterdeck behind the conning tower. The weapon was for our defense while our submarine was on the surface.

Since I had never pulled that watch assignment before, I hot-footed it to one of the gunner's mates, a sailor who took care of that gun, to find out what I was expected to do when we went to "Battle Stations, Gun Action."

He told me that I would have padded gloves and, when the shell casing came out of the weapon after firing, I would be expected to catch the hot casing so it would not bounce around on the deck and hurt someone.

Chapter 51

Hot Shot!

*"Tell the men to fire faster.
Fight 'til she sinks, Boys.
Don't give up the ship!"*
Captain James Lawrence
US Navy, June 1813

The next day, after getting underway and being in our proper operating area, the *Conger* submerged. Suddenly, the alarm sounded.

"Battle Stations, Gun Action!" the boat's loudspeakers blared.

As soon as it was announced, I reported to the Control Room where I was given two large padded gloves and told to stand by. We surfaced and the gun crew went up on deck.

I went to the back of the gun and stood by. The weapon moorings were loosened and the men took their stations to fire this large cannon.

I was standing by and ready to catch the hot shell casing after the gun fired.

The men were pointing the gun's muzzle at a predetermined target until orders eventually came down from the bridge.

"Commence firing!" the Captain bellowed.

Well, the gun fired and that, in itself, scared me nearly to death. But no one told me that the hot shell casing would be discharged when the gun barrel went forward following the recoil, not immediately after the shell was fired.

I instinctively put my gloved hands up to catch the spent shell. Nothing happened as the gun barrel traveled backwards. When the gun barrel started moving forward, however, out popped the still-steaming shell casing. It bounced on the deck and then tumbled over the side of our boat and into the water.

All I could do was watch as it plunged, still hissing, beneath the ocean's waves.

The same thing happened on the gun's second firing. Then we secured the cannon and all of us returned below from our Battle Stations, Gun Action.

The Chief of the Boat, the senior enlisted man onboard — and at that moment in time, God, as far as I was concerned — told me in clipped sentences that my days as a "hot shell" man were now over.

Chapter 52

Getting Qualified Redux

I busied myself for the remainder of the *Conger*'s sea trials in getting qualified in submarines.

This was a large undertaking.

To qualify, a crew member had to know and understand each and every system and valve arrangement in the entire submarine. I did this by preparing a notebook and drawing the systems and electrical circuits in that notebook. When I had learned a system or circuit, I took the drawing to a leading petty officer and he would quiz me. If he was convinced of my expertise, he would sign me off.

I continued this exercise throughout the entire submarine. When I had all the systems signed off, I presented my completed notebook to the Chief of the Boat.

When he was satisfied, he sent me to the Engineering Officer, who took me through the entire boat, quizzing me as we went.

After three or four hours, when he was satisfied, he declared me qualified in submarines.

Chapter 53

Wetting My Dolphins

"These dolphins, once you pin them on your chest, leave deep marks right over your heart long after the uniforms have been put away."
Bud F. Turner, ex-MT2(SS)
USS Stonewall Jackson (SSBN-634)
Gold Crew, Plank Owner

Once I met all of the requirements for qualification, the Chief Petty Officer presented me with a pair of cloth dolphins that I stitched onto the lower part of my uniform's right sleeve.

Top: cloth dolphins.   Bottom: silver metal pin

Years later, placement of those cloth dolphins was transferred to the upper left breast of the uniform. A couple of years after that, we were authorized to wear silver-plated metal dolphins on the left breast of our uniform shirts in place of the cloth dolphins.

After I was qualified, the next time I went topside some members of the crew threw me over the side. This practice was called wetting your dolphins and is a time-honored tradition in the submarine force.

About this same time, I was advanced from Fireman's Apprentice with an E-2 rating to Fireman with an E-3 rating. That meant another raise in pay.

During this period in my career, all submariners received their normal pay plus an 80 percent differential for hazardous duty.

By 1952, President Harry Truman and the Democrat-controlled US Congress decided to give submariners a pay raise but also instituted a flat rate scale with no submariner differential. This meant I was actually reduced in pay by $31 a month.

I have been a Republican ever since.

James Gibson, submarine qualified!

Chapter 54

Atlantic Coast Duty

*"A good Navy is not a provocation to war.
It is the surest guaranty of peace."*
President Theodore Roosevelt

About this time, too, the powers that be realized that the submarines of Squadron Six, including the *USS Conger*, were on the West Coast or Pacific Ocean side of the Panama Canal but all of our training took place in the Atlantic Ocean.

This meant that every time there was a training exercise, we would first have to transit the canal.

Transiting the Panama Canal meant sailors not on duty or working had a lot of fun whenever the boat stopped for swim call and sun bathing in Gatun Lake, midway through the canal.

On a more serious note, however, each of those transits was a monumental waste of fuel oil and took time away from our actual training.

Submarine Squadron 6, now part of Commander Submarines Atlantic Fleet, was transferred, along with our submarine tender ship *Orion* and all of our squadron's staff personnel, to Norfolk, Virginia, our new home port.

In route to Norfolk, we were in a very detailed operation to simulate a real war patrol. We made a torpedo approach on the aircraft carrier *USS Midway*. That meant we had to submerge and get through the *Midway*'s defensive screen of several destroyers. We did so by staying submerged for more than 36 hours and were successful in simulating the sinking of that mighty carrier.

In staying submerged for that period of time, though, we used up almost all of our boat's oxygen.

Those crew members who had missed combat operations during World War II finally understood what it had been like for the wartime submarines and crews to do so time and again. When attacked by enemy forces, whether from air, sea or shore, the safest place to continue a patrol was for a submarine to remain submerged for many hours at a time.

While underwater, however, none of us could even light a cigarette as there was so little oxygen remaining in the submarine.

Also, after several hours of breathing such oxygen-depleted air, it often took me several minutes and a lot of exertion to open just one of our large sea suction valves to provide more cooling water for the engines, a chore that under normal circumstances would have taken no more than a minute or two.

Chapter 55

Time Out
for Sports

When the war exercise was completed, the *Conger* and the *USS Runner* (SS-476) each made port visits to the US Navy Base at Guantanamo Bay, Cuba.

As was the custom at the time, whenever two submarines shared the same port, the junior vessel's crew would furnish the beer for an intra-ship softball game. Whichever crew's team lost the game, that ship wound up paying for the beer.

Win or lose, however, all who played or watched the game were able to enjoy the ice-cold libations.

On most boats, the hospital corpsman was also the athletic officer, along with his regular medical duties. So our Executive Officer called the Doc up to his stateroom.

"Order the beer for a baseball game," the skipper told the Doc.

Our Doc had never been in Cuba before, so figuring

that there would be 60 sailors at most attending the game, Doc went to the Base Exchange and ordered six cases of local beer to be delivered to the recreation field where the ball game was to be played.

What Doc didn't know was that the local beer in Cuba was Cerveza Hatuey, a Cuban-style ale that contained more alcohol that most wines.

Even worse, the beer bottles were packed 90 to a case.

Needless to say, there were a lot of out-of-control sailors that day. On top of that, no one remembered or even cared which team won the game.

Chapter 56

Underway Training

"Earning your dolphins is what signifies to the rest of the crew that you can and will be trusted with our lives. I couldn't imagine trusting my life and the life of the boat with anyone I didn't know personally. If you're on my boat and you're wearing dolphins, then I trust you. Period. I don't care if you're a yoeman, cook, missile technician or mechanic — I know you've got my back. It doesn't get any more intimate than that."
Joseph Brugeman, ET2, US Navy
The Silent Service: Submarine Duty
Written by Rod Powers

As usual, I was shaken from these pleasant reveries to attend to pressing tasks aboard the *Coucal*.

Once freed from handling sensitive assignments, we spent much of our time during deployment to WestPac as part of the Commander Pacific Fleet Training Group.

While serving in this elite group, they trained our ship and crew in all ship-board evolutions. The trainers also scrutinized how well or poorly the crew and I reacted to their various training practices.

During the underway phases of fleet training, we were required to exercise our ship in several drills including a simulation of a man overboard, a ship-to-ship collision, fires in various sections of our ship, a medical emergency or two, and, of course, our gunnery skills.

The *USS Coucal* was classed as an auxiliary type vessel, so she was very limited as to her guns. We did, however, have four 50 caliber machine guns mounted at various points on the deck and superstructure, as well as lots of hand-held weapons.

During these training evolutions, our ship was ordered to man battle stations. One of our ship's cooks was the machine gun operator. To simulate a target, we threw an empty 50 gallon drum over the side and brought the ship out to about 500 yards from the target.

"Commence Firing!" was ordered and, believe it or not, our cook hit the floating drum with his second round. Low and behold, the drum sank out of sight. As a result of that performance, the *USS Coucal* was recognized as having the highest gunnery score for auxiliary ships in the entire Pacific Fleet.

We also came through the rest of our training with flying colors. *Coucal* was rated outstanding in all departments and one of the most cooperative ships the fleet trained that year.

Whether participating in fleet exercises or on our own, I and the ship's officers continued our own crew's training while doing routine onboard maintenance. It wasn't long before the *USS Coucal* was becoming known as a proud unit of Commander Submarine Pacific and the entire Pacific fleet.

The ship was given an overall grade of outstanding. More to my own satisfaction was the fact that we were trained and functioning as an outstanding unit of Commander Submarines Pacific.

Major credit for upgrading the *Coucal* was due to the high caliber of people on Commander Submarine Squadron Three's staff.

In particular, I must single out the efforts of Lieutenant Michael Tiernan, now a retired Captain. Then, however, Mike was the

Squadron Engineer Officer. As such, Mike controlled our repair and habitability funds. When he took notice of our own efforts to improve the ship as well as the skills of our crew, he stepped forward and offered to help us in every way he could.

Well, ever since my boot camp days of eating off of steel mess trays, that has always been a sore spot. On board the *Coucal*, we were staffed with people who could not only fix things but they could also install items.

With Lieutenant Michael Tiernan's permission, we went to a nearby town and ordered the manufacture of a holder for stainless steel meat platters that could dispense steam-warmed meat platters. We also went about replacing the steel trays from which our crew members had to eat their meals.

Instead, we started serving platters of food to each table for family style dining. It wasn't long before we also upgraded the crew's dining area. For this job, the Pearl Harbor Submarine Base Repair Department stepped forward in a very helpful manner when we sought their assistance.

Chapter 57

Rescue Missions

About this time, the *Coucal* was ordered to Hilo, a city on the big island of Hawaii. It was partly a show of the nation's flag, but also a chance for our crew to take some liberty ashore.

While en route that night, the Boatswain Mate of the Watch reported that he observed what he thought might be a red emergency signal flare off our starboard side.

No one else saw it, but I was on the bridge and thought I might have had a slight glimpse of something similar.

Anyway, we turned towards where he had first reported seeing the flare. We continued on that same heading for quite a while and we were very nearly ready to turn back to our original course when suddenly, and without question, this time we each observed another red flare lighting up a small patch of the night sky.

Eventually, the *Coucal*'s crew rescued three fishermen who were hopelessly lost.

The engine in their boat would not start and they were adrift. Much earlier, they had been anchored closer to shore and in shallow water. But somehow, they had made a serious error in judgment and pulled up the anchor before starting their engine.

When the engine failed to start, they were now drifting out to sea in water deeper than their anchor line.

Once we had them safely on board the *Coucal*, they told us that they had nearly given up hope of being rescued. They were completely out of fresh water and down to the very last of their emergency signal flares.

At this point, we took their boat in tow and continued on our way.

Upon our arrival in Hilo, the fishermen we rescued and other citizens of Hilo feted us to several parties. No *Coucal* sailor could purchase a drink because everyone there wanted to treat us.

Our stay in Hilo concluded a very fine weekend port visit.

To add to the trip's excitement and to top off that weekend, while we were steaming back towards Pearl Harbor, we spotted a sail boat that had capsized.

The surrounding seas were too rough for the *Coucal* to maneuver very close to the sailboat without causing serious damage to the overturned craft.

However, we observed several people safely resting on top of the keel of the overturned sail boat, so we stood by until the US Coast Guard arrived. The sailboat's crew of four were eventually rescued, the sailboat righted and placed in tow.

Once again, the *Coucal* was capably doing her secondary job in rescuing people at sea.

Chapter 58

Kudos to the *Coucal*

Upon the *Coucal*'s return to Pearl Harbor, we were placed under the tactical command of the Pacific Anti-Submarine Warfare Command for three weeks. This time period was for that command to use ships from a variety of other commands to conduct a classified operation at sea.

Due to the extreme sensitivity of those times, however, our reports were deemed classified and remain so today.

We came through this evolution in fine stead and we were commended at several levels of command.

Commendation
Commander Antisubmarine Warfare Force, U.S. Pacific Fleet
Takes Pleasure in Commending
Lieutenant Commander James W. Gibson, United States Navy
For service as set forth in the following
CITATION
For meritorious service as Commanding Officer, USS Coucal (ASR-8), while participating as a unit of Task Group 30.5 during the period 4 March through 19 March 1970.

You consistently displayed an exceptionally high degree of professionalism, excellent seamanship and devotion to duty while performing assigned duties in an operation of great importance to improving the defense posture of the United States.

Your dedication, resourcefulness and initiative reflect great credit to yourself and the manner by which your ship performed assigned duties is an indication of outstanding personal achievement and competence.

Signed: *E.P. AURAND*
VICE ADMIRAL, US NAVY
Commander, Antisubmarine Warfare Force
US Pacific Fleet

Later the *Coucal* also received the Navy's Meritorious Unit Commendation with a ribbon to be worn on our uniforms. Not too bad for a 30-year-old ship that used to be severely ridiculed as a poor performer and barely capable of getting underway without mishap.

The Secretary of the Navy
takes pleasure in presenting the
MERITORIOUS UNIT COMMENDATION
to
TASK GROUP 30.5
for service as set forth in the following:
CITATION:
For meritorious service during the periods 27 August to 15 November 1969 and 13 January to 30 March 1970, while executing a highly complex operation in the Pacific Ocean, which demanded precise

coordination between elements on the sea and ashore.

Through their professionalism, remarkable seamanship and dedication, the officers and crew members of the ships and land support counterparts of Task Group 30.5 successfully executed a sensitive mission which was vital to the defense of the nation.

Their continuous display of fine judgment, resourcefulness and willingness to work many long hours on a sustained basis made possible the completion of the assigned tasks which resulted in a most important contribution to the increased anti-submarine warfare capability of the United States.

By their perseverance and unfailing devotion to duty throughout this period, the personnel of Task group 30.5 upheld the highest traditions of the United States Naval Service.

For the Secretary,

E. R. Zumwalt, Jr.

Admiral, United States Navy

Chief of Naval Operations

About this time, a sister ship, the *USS Greenlet* (ASR-10), returned from WestPac and was also moored at the Pearl Harbor Submarine Base. In a short time, she was to be turned over to the Turkish Navy and re-christened as *TCG Akin* (A-585) with Commander Necdet Donertas as skipper.

During the turn-over refitting, the *Coucal* acted as host ship for the *TCG Akin*'s stay in Hawaii. As part of our show of hospitality, the crew of the *Coucal* hosted a picnic for the *Akin*'s crew at Kehee

Lagoon. Amidst the feasting, revelry and storytelling, it was decided that the captains of each ship should compete in a foot race. I'm not sure how it happened, but the race was eventually declared a draw.

This just goes to show that I could not win them all!

Chapter 59

Medical Emergency

As one might suspect, life does go on for family members left behind.

While serving aboard the *Conger* shortly after I first qualified for submarine duty, the boat was reassigned to the East Coast. After stopping at Guantanamo Bay in Cuba, we also stopped for a brief port visit at the Submarine Base in Key West, Florida.

Shortly after arrival, I received a telegram from the Red Cross. My mother was hospitalized in New Castle, Penn. As the telegram indicated, Sarah Belle was in a very serious condition. Already diagnosed with diabetes, Mom had contracted diabetic gangrene in her right foot.

The Chief of the Boat immediately sent me home on emergency leave.

Mom recovered without losing her legs, thanks in large part to Dr. Dave Perry. He used a very innovative technique for that time by bathing the leg with light from an ultraviolet lamp. The UV rays destroyed the infection. That was revolutionary medicine in those days.

After a few days helping my Mother at home, I reported back to the *USS Conger*, now berthed in Norfolk, Virginia. Incidentally, that trip involved my first ride on a commercial airplane. Capitol Airlines flew me from Pittsburgh to Norfolk.

Chapter 60

Armed Forces Day Parade

During our port time stay, the *USS Conger* was ordered to travel to Newport News, Virginia, where it was invited to be a visiting submarine for that city's Armed Forces Day celebration.

Furthermore, the senior officer of our submarine base sent over word that the *Conger* was to provide a marching unit for a parade scheduled during the boat's Newport News visit.

Sailors, especially those on submarines, are not ideally suited to be in a drill team. As luck would have it, our boat was moored alongside an out-of-commission aircraft carrier, so we did our best and practiced marching drills on the deserted aircraft carrier's flight deck.

To be honest, even with the additional marching practice we still weren't very good.

On Armed Forces Day, before the parade started, our designated assembly point was right in front of a local bar. To make matters worse, the beer was "on the house" for our group.

Being sailors, you can imagine what happened next.

Well, we started heading down the parade route following directly behind a Marine Corps drill team.

Our guys were out of step. And every once in a while, one of our sailors would slip out of ranks to grab a good looking girl and give her a hug.

As the Marines marched by, the crowd politely clapped. But when the *Coucal*'s sailors sauntered by, the crowd went wild in clapping and hollering for us.

Of course we were all in trouble by the time we got back to the boat.

On the captain's orders, we slipped our moorings and quietly returned to our berthing in Norfolk.

Chapter 61

Special Ops in the Arctic North

"The North Atlantic is a cruel and unforgiving body of water."
Thomas Barnhart
Senior Chief Machinists Mate
USS City of Corpus Christi

USS Conger was one of the first submarines to conduct special operations in the Northern Atlantic Ocean, well north of the Arctic Circle. During this particular deployment, the United States was using its submarine fleet to collect classified information regarding Russia's naval operations. This was at the beginning of what was eventually termed the Cold War.

We were ordered to observe sea conditions of that area of the North Atlantic. However, the *Conger* did not have a snorkel, a retractable air intake and exhaust pipe that enabled its diesel engines to operate while the submarine was submerged to a periscope depth of 58 feet.

The Germans had invented a snorkeling system during World War II. The snorkel that was eventually put on some American submarines allowed those boats to run their powerful diesel engines just below the surface for greater propulsion or while charging the boat's batteries thus supplying fresh sea air for the boat's crew to breathe.

We learned quickly that the Atlantic Ocean is almost always very choppy and rough. Our trip was at the start of winter, so it was also very cold. I stood some of my duty watches while we were on the surface.

As the lookout, I spent a great deal of time topside, standing beside the periscope housing shears that extended above the bridge deck.

It was so cold that those of us on deck watch could only endure the icy blasts of sea spray and wind for 20 minutes at a time before we had to be helped below decks for a warming cup of coffee.

Chapter 62

Diesel Fumes and Oil Stains

When not on lookout watch during this same north Atlantic operation, I worked shifts in the *Conger*'s forward engine-room.

While running on the surface, air for our submarine and its crew came directly from topside through the main induction valve's 36-inch opening just behind the conning tower. That air was dumped into the engine-rooms and distributed from there throughout the boat.

While working my shifts in the engine-room, I ended up wearing the same foul weather clothing I wore topside just to keep warm.

It was also very cold throughout the boat because the boat's electric space heaters used too much power and were never turned on. The *Conger*'s battery power had to be preserved so we could use them for propulsion whenever the boat submerged.

When the *Conger* eventually returned to Norfolk, I started to look for a new home that might be somewhat warmer.

In other words, I sought assignment to a submarine heading for the West Coast with porting in sunny San Diego.

Chapter 63

California Bound

The good Lord was on the job. There happened to be just such a boat transferring to San Diego. The *USS Spinax* (SSR–489) was leaving in a few weeks for sunny California. Better yet, it just so happened that there was a man on the *Spinax* with the same rating and job classification as mine. Better yet, he wanted to remain in Norfolk.

Not much later, I found myself on the *Spinax*, making way for the Pacific Ocean fleet.

Once again we cruised through the Panama Canal. During this passage, I was standing plenty of engine-room watches and was soon advanced to Engineman Third Class with a rank of E-4.

USS Spinax (SSR - 489) underway.   US Navy Photo

That promotion meant I was now a petty officer and had earned yet another pay raise.

When the *Spinax* stopped in Acapulco, Mexico, for a port visit, many crew members were given liberty. But since I had security watch duty, I stayed below decks while the boat was in port.

A torpedoman by the name of Woods came back from being on shore liberty and wanted to borrow $20 from me.

"What are you going to do with the money?" I asked him.

"I have a date with a Miss Griesedieck," he replied.

Based on his pronunciation of her last name, I immediately surmised this was most likely a con job and told him he had to find the $20 elsewhere.

To my chagrin, a few years later I found out that there actually was a person by that name and she was an heiress to the Falstaff Beer fortune.

Chapter 64

Casting the Leads

Upon arriving in San Diego, I had my first encounter with avocados. I thought they had no taste and were a complete waste of money and time. Eventually I learned to like them. Now I can't get enough of them.

The *USS Spinax* was a good boat and I made several longtime friends among the crew. I still see some of my former crew members whenever we get together at various submariner reunions or the national conventions sponsored by the United States Submarine Veterans Inc.

One such person was Bob Tift, now retired with the rank of Chief Petty Officer. When I first got to know him, Bob was a Gunners Mate with the rank of Second Class Petty Officer.

During World War II, most submarines had deck guns and carried other weapons on board. The Gunners Mates took care of these weapons and repaired them.

Anyway, while still in Norfolk and just prior to leaving for San Diego, we were returning to port from a daily operation. At that time, the *Spinax* had a Lieutenant who served as our navigator. He kept track of where the boat was at any given time whenever the submarine was underway. His job was to keep us from running aground.

I guess this particular officer wanted to teach his men how things were done in the surface ship Navy. So he placed "Gunner" Tift on the bow of our boat to cast the leads. This was a way of measuring the water's depth beneath the hull with a 75-foot line at the end of which was tied a heavy sash weight.

At regular intervals along the line, different items are fastened to indicate a certain depth. For example, a piece of leather might indicate 25 feet while a shoe lace might indicate 50 feet.

The caster is stationed on the bow and throws the line out. All this time the boat continues underway as the lead and line plummet towards the bottom. If the bottom is less than 75 feet, one of the items tied to the line will show itself on the surface and the caster reports that to the bridge.

For example, "I have the bottom by the piece of leather!" would mean there was 25 feet of water below the hull.

By the same token, if the depth is too great, the line will hang straight down indicating there is plenty of water under the submarine. This evolution was rarely accomplished or even attempted on submarines.

Anyway, Tift was going along with this entire charade.

Whenever the bridge lookout would call down, "The bottom, where away?" Tift would respond, "No bottom!"

This went on for a while and each time the bridge was given the same response to the question "The bottom, where away?"

"No bottom!"

Finally, after several tries, a different answer came from the boat's bow.

"I have the bottom by the green rag!" Tift bellowed.

From the bridge came the response, "There is no green rag!"

To which Gunner Tift replied, "There ain't no friggin' bottom!"

Chapter 65

Horse and Cow

During my stay on the *Spinax*, I became a throttle man in the forward engine room because with every advance in rank there is more pay as well as greater responsibility. After operating out of San Diego for some time, we entered Hunter's Point Naval Shipyard located in San Francisco.

We were ordered there for a routine overhaul of four to six months duration to make major repairs and a complete overhaul of the *Tench*-class submarine originally commissioned in 1946.

I quickly learned from my shipmates that San Francisco was at that time the home of a very famous submariner watering hole or bar called The Horse and Cow. Most old time submariners visited that den of iniquity at least once just for the experience.

It was common for enlisted submariners who had recently earned their dolphins to gather at the Horse and Cow for a wetting ceremony. The dolphin pins were dropped into the bottom of a large pitcher, and then every manner of beer or liquid spirits were poured in to fill the container.

The submariner fraternity's new inductee would then be enticed to drink the pitcher until he could retrieve the dolphins. Only at that point would he truly be accepted by the gathered brethren.

Horse and Cow rules prohibit any kind words for the nuclear missile submarines known as boomers, and beware any non-submariners who might find themselves in the bar.

It was common knowledge that if you picked a fight with any submariner, you would have to fight them all.

I must admit that I frequented the bar often.

In 1959, The Horse and Cow moved from Hunter's Point to Vallejo, and later to San Diego. Today, it has again followed the submarine fleet to Bremerton, Washington.

Chapter 66

Back on the Gridiron

One afternoon while berthed in the shipyard, I and two other shipmates were called up to the barge where the ship's office and crew's barracks were temporarily housed while the *Spinax* was in overhaul.

This was not a normal routine during working hours for an enlisted man to be called to the barge, so I was worried as to what I might have done wrong.

I knew I had been seen going on liberty to San Francisco. But as best I knew, I had not yet run afoul of the Shore Patrol.

When I got to the barge, I was brought before a US Naval Captain, a huge Commander and a Lieutenant, a former Chief Petty Officer whom I had known back in San Diego. The Lieutenant was Tim McCoy, an ex-prisoner of war captured by the Japanese and a character mentioned in the must-read book titled *No Ordinary Joes*.

The large Commander was "Big Daddy" Don Whitmire, a former All-American in the 1940s while attending Mississippi State and again at the US Naval Academy.

The Captain was Slade Cutter, a 1936 graduate of the US Naval Academy. While there, he was an All-American football player and boxer. During World War II , Cutter was the Commanding Officer of the *USS Sea Horse* (SS-304) and the holder of four Navy

Crosses, two Silver Stars, a Bronze Star medal and a Presidential Unit Citation.

"Where did you play football?" Captain Cutter asked me.

I recounted my experiences playing with the Wabash Bears and Great Lakes teams.

The three officers informed us they intended to build a football team for the Navy's Submarine Force Pacific that would compete with teams from other Navy commands on the West Coast.

I and the two other sailors selected were told to travel to San Diego and try out for the team. Each of us made the team and we were in very select company indeed. This was during the Korean War and all the Armed Services were filling their depleted ranks with reservists.

Our team had five players who later played professionally in the National Football League. There were also several former first-team college players.

I ended up making the team as a third-string offensive guard. This was quite a thrill for a farm boy from Pennsylvania to be on the same team as those more accomplished players. During our time together, I was able to get into a couple of games for one or more plays.

But in our practice sessions, I was used mostly as cannon fodder for the starters. In other words, I ended up getting a lot of grass stains on my nose while at the Navy practice field off 5th Street on San Diego Naval Base.

Chapter 67

Moonlighting for C&H Sugar

After returning to the *USS Spinax* and a trip to Hawaii, along with operations out of Pearl Harbor, a request came out for men to go to Mare Island Naval Shipyard located at Vallejo.

The men selected were needed to put a new submarine, the *K-2*, now referred to as the *USS Bass* (SSK-2), in commission. This submarine was to be one of a class of K for Killer submarines known initially as *K-1, K-2* and *K-3*.

I was selected to join the *K-2* crew, so I proceeded on orders to Mare Island.

When several of us reported in to Mare Island Submarine Administration (Sub-AD), we were told that we were there way too early and there wasn't much we could do. However, we did find some make-work projects to keep us occupied for a time. There were blue prints of the boat to catalog and some spare parts to put aside for loading onto the boat later.

In reality, most days all we did was mess around and then go on liberty at night.

That is until our money ran out, which happened early on for me as I had received advanced pay prior to my transfer to Mare Island. That meant that my regular pay was reduced until I could repay the advanced amount.

To compensate for my lack of funds, I joined several others and went over to Crocket, Calif., and found work at the C&H (California and Hawaii) Sugar Company. We worked from 4 p.m. to midnight unloading 100-pound bags of sugar from cargo vessels or loading them in railroad cars.

We did that for eight long hours every shift.

This work caused us to be in very fine physical shape. Better yet, we were paid at the end of each shift. We would then head back to Vallejo to start our liberty on the infamous Georgia Street.

This street, better known as the Strip to most World War II submariners, was still carrying on as wildly as before well into the 1950s and '60s.

The numerous bars were always open until 2 a.m. Almost everyone in the submarine force between 1941 and 1960 knew of Georgia Street. And most of them roamed the many watering holes and strip clubs there.

The Strip had everything that a sailor could want after a long sojourn at sea. It was a totally "sailors only" area with all of the trimmings.

The Strip's notoriety started well before World War II and the building of ships, especially submarines. These same World War II-era submarines would also arrive there for periodic overhaul or battle repairs.

The sailors returning from those battle areas and war patrols used Georgia Street as an area to let off steam. They knew all to well that they would soon be returning to dangerous waters in a life-threatening environment.There are many stories of Vallejo and the Strip that could fill a book.

Chapter 68

Time to Re-Enlist

"The Navy is much more than a job, much more than service to country. It's a way of life. It gets in your blood."

Albert F. Pratt
Assistant Secretary of the Navy,
Personnel and Reserve Forces
(Sept. 1954 — Jan. 1957)

The *K-2* was designed to be a coastal defense submarine.

It had three small main engines that drove three generators that powered two main motors providing propulsion for the boat. These small engines were originally made to be auxiliary engines on fleet type submarines for powering auxiliary generators.

They were a constant headache for the K boats and particularly the engine room sailors assigned to keep them running.

We spent hours changing the spring packs that connect engines to generators. These spring packs were designed to take up the shock when you changed engine speed, but they were much too small for the amount of torque that these powerful engines applied.

During this time, the Korean War, known then as a police action, was in full bloom.

Commissioning ceremony of the *USS Bass* (SSK-2) in 1951

My enlistment was about to expire when President Truman extended all enlistments for one year. I already had three years in the Navy and was now a Third Class Petty Officer at the age of 21.

Since there was really nothing to go home to as far as a job was concerned, I reenlisted for six more years. As a result of my re-enlistment, I was granted home leave for 30 days.

While visiting my family back in Pennsylvania, I purchased a used car. My prize was a dark green 1948 Chrysler Highlander Windsor convertible. It had wood paneling on both sides and the seats were covered with a tartan plaid. I was ever so proud of that automobile and ended up driving it across the country when it was time for me to return to California.

Upon returning to Mare Island and the famous Navy Cafe, I sat down at the bar next to a fair damsel of Georgia Street for some proper venting.

She leaned over and whispered in my ear.

"You'd best get those dolphins off your chest before a submariner takes them off," she said slyly.

"Miss, I'll have you know I am a properly qualified submariner," I said, very proud of my status.

"No, you're not," she countered.

"You don't smell like diesel fuel!" she retorted with derision.

She was right. While I was visiting back home in Pennsylvania, my Mother washed all of my clothes and had my uniforms dry cleaned. Hence, there was no lingering smell of the boat in evidence.

With the *USS Bass* still under construction, I tried out for the Mare Island Area baseball team. I pitched and played first base for the Islanders. We played other teams in the 12th Naval District.

In fact, we were the 1951 champions of the 12th Naval District and I was selected to play on the All-District team.

Little did I know that something else was soon going to change my life forever forward.

Chapter 69

Chance Encounter

Later that same fall of 1951, two buddies and I happened to attend a local high school football game where I chanced to meet a girl. It was a cool mid-October Saturday evening and we were out to have a bit of fun.

We did not know it, but we ended up sitting in the red and white Vallejo High School rooting section. The Vallejo Apaches, later changed to Redhawks in 2014, were that very night playing their arch rivals, the blue-and-gold Indians from Napa High School.

Of course we were rooting for Napa.

This got quite a reaction from three young women sitting behind us. From their reaction, I guessed they must all be residents of Vallejo.

As the game ended, we asked the girls where they were heading. They mentioned that they were heading to Mel's Drive-In nearby.

Well, we just to happened to end up going to that very same restaurant. We three men were sitting in my convertible and, of course, the car's top was down.

We eventually caught the girls' attention and invited them to come over and have a soda with us all sitting in the convertible. The evening of Oct. 13, 1951, ended when the sodas were through, but there is much more to the story of that meeting than a first acquaintance.

Chapter 70

Fate Steps In

Low and behold, when Monday arrived, I went up on the base to the Supply Department to return a miss-sent part. There, seated at the desk marked Returns was the same girl with the shoulder-length dark brown hair who had caught my eye just two nights before.

And she was sitting at the very desk where I needed to discuss my problem about the part.

I proceeded to get in an argument with her and heated words were exchanged until her supervisor came over to settle things down. By this time I had found out the girl's name was Mary Lou.

Later I found out her full name was Mary Louise Buckthought, but she preferred going simply by Lou.

Out of a clear blue sky, I turned to the young lady and asked her if she would like to go out with me that same evening.

Much to my surprise, Lou said yes.

Chapter 71

Mary Louise Buckthought

A native of Grass Valley, Mary Lou had moved with her parents, Frederick Cecil and Myrtle May Buckthought, to Vallejo when she was a child of 9.

Her father quickly found a job as a machinist at the Mare Island Naval Shipyard and her Mother worked in the Solano County Assessor's Office. Her Dad played organ most evenings and weekends for the local Masonic Lodge.

"Vallejo was a sailor's town, and most of the high school girls learned early on that you didn't date sailors if you wanted to preserve your reputation," Mary Lou recalls.

Mary Lou's connection to the Masonic Lodge drew her to join the International Order of Rainbow for Girls when she was just 13. The service club for young women offered a drill team that marched in various parades. They also appeared at events throughout Northern California, as well as attended regional, district and national conventions.

At age 18 and a recent high school graduate, Mary Lou decided to quit her job working in the office of a local clothing store in Vallejo and instead seek a typist's job at the Mare Island Naval Shipyard's Supply Depot.

Chapter 72

Allure of a Convertible

It was fate that drew Mary Lou and two of her Rainbow Girls drill team members to attend that mid-October high school football game where they chanced to meet three young men cheering for the hated rival of their beloved alma mater.

After the game, the three men then turned up at the girl's favorite after-game night spot, Mel's Drive-In.

A 1948 Chrysler Highlander Windsor convertible with wood paneling and tartan upholstery.

However, it was the sleek convertible that Jim Gibson was driving that helped soften some of the girls' ill feelings toward the young men, she said.

"Jim had a convertible, so we thought we were safe!" Mary Lou explained.

But when it turned out the three young men, all sailors, barely had a dollar between them to buy the girls their 10-cent soda pops, the rose quickly began to lose its allure, she recalled.

Until a fateful second meeting two days later at the Supply Depot.

That was when I asked Mary Lou for a date after our second meeting, and Mary Lou agreed to accompany me to a nice dinner in San Francisco.

We were in my car and I was very proud to be seen with this beautiful young woman.

That is, until I took a turn onto one of San Francisco's steepest streets. Back then the automatic transmission in that car was what they called fluid drive.

When I tried to go up that hill, the transmission was slipping real bad and the car would not climb. In fact, I had to put the car in reverse and back down the street. Talk about being embarrassed!

Anyway, that first date started a romance that has lasted more than 65 years.

Chapter 73

Whirlwind Romance

When Mary Lou and I met, we were each 5-feet, 9-inches tall in our stockings.

At 21, I weighed 220 pounds, but was quite solid with muscles honed by carrying sacks of sugar. I was also in training for the Navy Submarine Force Pacific's football team as well as playing for the Mare Island Area Islander's championship baseball team.

Mary Lou was more petite at 125 pounds, kept slim by the marching drills and activities from her Rainbow Girl drill team.

"I was intrigued by Jim because he had a shorter last name than mine," Lou recalled with a knowing smile.

During the next six months, there was a whirlwind of activity as Lou and I got better acquainted.

By Dec. 25, 1951, I had given Lou an engagement ring and on March 15, 1952, we were pronounced husband and wife.

Our marriage has lasted for 65 years and weathered 32 household moves, two boys now grown into men, and many miles of adventure and romance, Mary Lou noted.

Chapter 74

Sea Trials on the *Bass*

The *USS Bass* or *K-2* was launched on May 2, 1951. Once the construction work was finished, she was put through many dock-side trials until she was commissioned on November 16, 1951

The *K-2*, as we called her, was now ready for sea trials.

USS Bass (SSK-2) underway   US Navy photo

We cast off from the dock at the shipyard and headed for San Francisco Bay and out through the Golden Gate for open ocean. After passing under the bridge and beyond the Farallon Islands, we were in the Pacific Ocean.

We rigged the boat for its first ocean dive and cautiously submerged, all the while checking for leaks. All was deemed good.

Now it was time for our first test dive down to 412 feet.

All went well and we surfaced. We ran a few at-sea tests before heading back to San Francisco and a return to Mare Island. There we were scheduled for the submarine's final days of tests and completion of a short list of necessary repairs.

As we passed back under the Golden Gate Bridge and headed into San Francisco Bay, the boat was in a busy ship traffic channel going past Alcatraz Island and Angel Island.

However, the tide was running out towards the ocean and we were heading directly into it. The tide runs at about 4 knots on a full ebb in that part of the bay.

The *K-2*, even with her three GMC 8-268A engines, was extremely under-powered and could make only about 9 knots on a flat sea with no current.

Captain Bunting was on the bridge and our Engineering Officer Jeff Metezel, later a Rear Admiral, was on watch in the Maneuvering Room.

"Give me all you've got, Jeff. I am trying to keep her from heading back out to sea!" the Captain called down to Maneuvering on the 1MC speaker system.

Of course, our skipper said that in jest, but we knew from his statement that the submarine was very much underpowered.

Chapter 75

Permission Granted

Back at Mare Island Navy Ship Yard for some final touch-ups, Mary Louise Buckthought and I took the opportunity to get married.

Since this was still very much the old Navy and because I was only a Third Class Petty Officer, I had to gain my captain's permission to be married. So I went before the skipper and pleaded my case.

"The poor girl deserves better, but permission is granted," he declared with a smirk.

The wedding took place in Grass Valley, Mary Lou's birthplace, on March 15, 1952.

Mary Lou and I motored to Grass Valley on the day before the wedding and stayed in separate rooms at her grandmother's home.

After supper and some visiting, I was getting ready for bed.

As I climbed between the icy sheets, I let out a scream to which the family came running into the guest bedroom. After they put a warm brick in the bed beside me, I was able to get some sleep.

Lou and I were married the next day at the First Methodist Church.

The morning of our wedding, snow started to fall. By the time the ceremony was over, the snow was deep enough that I had to install tire chains so we could leave. Thus, we proceeded on for the first time together as husband and wife.

We financed our honeymoon on a lot of spare change that Mary Lou had saved over the years, along with some money that her folks had also saved for her.

When Lou started working at Mare Island after graduating from high school, she paid her parents $75 each month for rent from her earnings. Unbeknownst to Lou, instead of spending that money on household goods and groceries, her parents had placed the funds into a savings account for her honeymoon expenses.

At the wedding, Dad and Mom Buckthought presented Lou with a bank book showing the total amount of all of their deposits.

After the wedding, while traveling to Sacramento to spend our honeymoon night, I was driving a bit too fast through the small town of Rocklin, Calif., on the old route of US Highway 40.

This stretch of highway was well-known as a speed trap. Of course, I was pulled over.

The officer asked me whether I had seen the speed limit signs in his town?

"I hadn't even noticed the town," I said, cracking wise

My ill-advised remark cost me a precious $10.

Chapter 76

Hawaii, Here We Come

When we returned from our honeymoon, I reported back to Vallejo's Mare Island shipyards where the *K-2* was finishing up with all of her sea trials and pre-underway tests.

The submarine was by now officially accepted by the US Navy.

In April, this brand new submarine set sail for Pearl Harbor, Hawaii, her new home port, with me on board.

My bride Mary Lou, however, stayed behind in Vallejo with her parents.

Back then, you had to be a Second Class Petty Officer with a rank of E-5 for the Navy to move your family and your belongings at their expense.

Of course ,we did not have that kind of money to bring Mary Lou to Hawaii on commercial transportation. However, by the time the *K-2* arrived at Pearl Harbor, I had made the rank of Engineman Second Class with an E-4 rating.

Now, finally, Mary Lou could join me in Hawaii at the Navy's expense.

I do remember writing to Lou and telling her of my new rating. I also told her that with my Second Class Petty Officer's pay, along with the hazardous duty supplement that went along with submarine duty, we would be taking home about $250 a month.

"If we could not make it on that, we should have our butts kicked," I boasted to my bride.

So in June of 1952, my 18-year-old wife who had never really been farther away from home than Reno, Nevada, sailed from San Francisco on the *USNS Sergeant Charles E. Mower* (T-AP-186), a World War II troop transport ship that had been converted to carry military dependents between San Francisco and various Pacific Ocean islands including the Territory of Hawaii.

When Mary Lou arrived, we newlyweds set up housekeeping.

That is a story in itself.

Chapter 77

Sand Castles
and Motel Rooms

We rented a little place in Honolulu on Hobron Lane, near Waikiki Beach. Along with several other *K-2* folks, Lou and I rented a room in the Ala Moana Motel. We were able to secure a larger room with all the essentials including a double bed, a bathroom and a very small kitchen. The room rent was $70 a month for the other tenants, but ours was $75 because we had an extra window and received cross ventilation as there was no air conditioning back then.

The Ala Moana Hotel fronts Waikiki Beach in Honolulu, Hawaii

There were many good times while we were there. The ship's crew was all very close and our wives were able to depend on each other while their husbands were at sea. We spent a lot of time on Waikiki Beach when the submarine was in port.

During the time we lived there, Hawaii was not yet a state and was still considered a territory. Everything was pure island living.

We were not allowed to buy food at the local markets because of sanitary regulations. Vegetables, especially, were suspect because of the human fertilizer or night soil used in growing the plants.

The open-air markets also had fresh meat and raw chickens hanging from the front beams to attract customers. Of course we were able to use the Navy Commissary and the Navy Base Exchange.

At that time the only real department store on the whole island was Sears and Roebucks.

Before Lou arrived in Hawaii, I was able to purchase an old Pontiac sedan.

This is a very good time to tell you of Mary Lou's courage and tenacity. She is a first generation English immigrant.

The first time that I had to leave her and go to sea, we awoke and got ready. Then, I drove Lou to the Pearl Harbor Submarine Base where the *K-2* was docked.

The boat was getting underway that same morning for a week's worth of sea trials and training operations. We hugged and kissed at the gangway and then I started to board the boat.

"How do I get home?" she called after me.

"Drive the car home," I hollered back.

I knew that she had completed a driver's training course while in high school and she had successfully obtained a driver's license, but she did not yet have a lot of driving practice in city traffic.

She not only drove herself home, but she and the car met me at the pier when the *K-2* returned from its time at sea.

Not only that, but Mary Lou quickly became the designated driver for many shopping, sightseeing and beach outings with other submarine wives whenever I went on a cruise.

Chapter 78

Playing Tourist

Whenever the *USS Bass* was in port, there were a great many things for the two of us to do and see. We did a lot of sightseeing all around Oahu. Back on base, there were softball games and stock car races were held in the baseball stadium, inside the fence and on the outfield.

The cars were jalopies that never went more than 30 – 35 miles an hour. There were lots of wrecks and seeing them was even more fun.

For a Sunday drive, we would venture up the old and very crooked and ever so steep road up over the Pali Pass to the windward side of Oahu.

If you have ever watched movies of the Japanese surprise attack on Pearl Harbor on December 7, 1941, the Pali Pass is where the first Japanese airplanes came over the hills to start their attack on the American ships moored below.

We were together in Hawaii for about four months until October, when I received orders to transfer to the Severn River Naval Command at Annapolis, Maryland.

This was to be my first assigned shore duty.

Chapter 79

Flying on
Marina Mars

Lou and I were very excited because we would be together more. We would also be on the East Coast and close by a lot of famous sites for our weekend adventures.

In getting ready to proceed and execute my transfer orders, a friend of mine made special arrangements for Mary Lou and I to travel back to the United States together by air.

It happened that the friend of a friend secured us a ride on a Navy seaplane that would carry us to the Alameda Naval Air Station (NAS) located on San Francisco Bay. It was to be on a giant flying boat, the *Marina Mars*.

At the time, the *Marina Mars* was one of the largest airplanes in the world. It was so large that it had an upper and lower deck and that was unheard of back then.

The *Marina Mars* taking off   US Navy photo

The day came for us to say good bye to the *K-2* and our shipmates and friends. By then, I had sold our car and what few odds and ends we had acquired in Hawaii to some of my shipmates.

A day or two later, we arrived at the pier to board the plane. After checking our luggage and confirming our ticketed passage, we boarded the large float plane. Oh, was it ever a big airplane!

And this was to be Lou's first ride on a plane. We went on board and were seated, but after just a few minutes all the passengers were ordered off and sent back to the pier.

We learned that a float on the plane's wing had come into contact with the pier and a small hole had been punched through the floatation chamber's skin. A maintenance crew was already patching the hole as we waited.

This didn't help Mary Lou's or my nerves.

After a short delay, we were told to re-board the seaplane and they again prepared us for take-off. The plane taxied out to the area where it was clear enough of boats so we could have plenty of space to gain lift and air speed.

Our seats were on the lower deck; the chiefs and officers were seated topside. We were seated by a porthole window close enough to the water so that the prop wash came back along the fuselage when the pilot increased power to the engines for takeoff.

We could see all this water flashing by outside our porthole. This had us both thinking that any hole in the floatation device they talked about before might be a bigger deal than they thought.

Thank goodness we soon had an up angle and took to the sky, leaving the surface of the ocean behind. Seriously, the takeoff did scare both of us.

Thirteen hours later we approached the San Francisco Bay Area and landed on the East Bay by Alameda Naval Air Station.

Chapter 80

Visiting Relatives

Mary Lou's folks met us at the dock in Alameda. After a lot of hugs and greetings between daughter and parents, sometime later we found our way back in Vallejo.

We stayed with Mary Lou's folks for a nice visit and brought them current on our adventures in Hawaii and about our flight back to the mainland.

A few days after buying an automobile, this time a 1941 Mercury, we ventured east. Many miles and a couple of flat tires in the middle of Utah later, we arrived at my folk's home in Mount Jackson, Pennsylvania.

Mary Lou was finally able to meet her in-laws, Sam and Sarah Belle Gibson, who had not been able to make it to our wedding.

It was a tearful yet joyous meeting and all of it happened in a very short moment. Of course, there had to be a party for the relatives to meet my new bride, after which we had a short but pleasant visit.

We said goodbye to Dad and Mom knowing we would be within driving distance for future visits and then we drove to Annapolis, Maryland, and my new duty station.

Chapter 81

Managing the Fleet

My new duty station was across the Severn River from the US Naval Academy. It was a support command made up of small boats and a fleet of sailing boats used by the boating programs taught at the US Naval Academy.

Being an engineman by training meant that I worked on the engines on both the small boats and the auxiliary engines aboard the larger sailing vessels. It was a very good tour for us being newly married.

We were close by Baltimore, Maryland, and Washington, DC.

We were also near my home in western Pennsylvania where we could visit my folks, which we did on several occasions. They were also able to come down and visit us in Annapolis.

During our stay there, Mary Lou found work in the secretarial pool for the Governor of Maryland's constituent services office where she helped out with income tax disputes and other issues.

Her paycheck was a welcome supplement to my Navy income since I had once again lost the additional pay for serving on a submarine.

The extra income allowed us some additional freedom on weekends when I did not have duty assignments or was not playing baseball.

We ventured several times to New York City and explored that city's then-famous Latin Quarter with plenty of eateries touting their beautiful yet scantily clad waitresses.

This was quite an eyeful for each of us.

Chapter 82

On the Mound

While in Annapolis, I was able to play baseball and basketball for our enlisted men's team. The Severn River Command had a very fine baseball team of which I was selected to be one of the starting pitchers.

We played in the Armed Forces Middle Atlantic League against teams from the Army, Air Force and Coast Guard. In the summer of 1954, our baseball team participated in the All Navy Tournament held that year in Norfolk, Va.

During that time, I was selected as an honorary "All-Navy" pitcher. Also, several of us sailors were invited to play for a civilian professional league team based out of Davidsonville, Md.

One day, I was pitching against a very good team, also from Maryland, that had several ex-Major League players on the squad.

One of those players was Babe Phelps, who had been a regular catcher for the Pittsburgh Pirates in the Major Leagues.

I had my pitches going good for me that day and I put Babe out three or four times. During his final chance at bat, I even struck him out.

As the game drew to a close, I couldn't keep my mouth shut.

As I passed Phelps, I casually said something to the effect, "Tough day, Babe?"

His response was terse.

"Yeah, Lefty, you were right on! But you don't throw a thing like Carl Hubble."

Carl Hubble was a great pitcher and a member of the Baseball Hall of Fame. He played for several years with the New York Giants, later the San Francisco Giants.

That was quite a put down to a less than great kid with a smart mouth.

Chapter 83

Sailing Vessels

Some weekends, I was required to sail on the fleet of the US Naval Academy's sailboats. Every year in those days there was a grand and very famous sailing event that took place in the Atlantic Ocean.

It was the Newport, Rhode Island, to Annapolis, Maryland, sail boat race.

Two sailboats from the US Naval Academy were entered in the 1952 race.

I was selected as the onboard engineman to cover any mechanical problems that might come up.

Royono yacht

It was quite a thrill to be involved in that endeavor, and also a lot of fun. Our boat the *Royono* won the over-all cup.

When John F. Kennedy became President, he purchased the *Royono* and converted it into a private yacht. Today, the *Royono* is based on San Francisco Bay.

In 1954, Hurricane Carol came calling along the East Coast. I rode out the storm on a very large sailboat, the *Freedom*. During the storm, there were very large waves even on the Severn River. It was scary, but we survived.

The sailing vessel *Freedom* was a prize of war brought back from Nazi Germany after World War II. It was more than 100 feet long and had a 109-foot main mast.

It had full living accommodations on board and even was outfitted with a bathtub at that time.

Chapter 84

Sick Leave and Paperwork

During my time in Annapolis, I was promoted to Engineman First class with an E-6 rating. This was quite unusual as I had only been in the Navy for five years.

Advancing that far in such a short time was almost unheard of in the peacetime Navy.

At that time, only three of the Second Class Enginemen with E-5 ratings serving in the Atlantic Fleet were promoted to First Class with an E-6 rating and I was one of them.

It was also during that same time period that Mary Lou nearly lost me. I ended up in the US Naval Academy Hospital with severe lead poisoning. This was caused from using gasoline to clean engine parts.

Fortunately, I came out of it with no lasting effects.

While stationed in Annapolis, I learned about another holdover tradition from the old Navy.

In order to take a day off from duty, a paper request was required. On the form, there had to be a valid excuse.

Married men had little or no trouble getting time off for family matters, but a single man wanting to go on liberty just to have a beer was not considered a valid excuse.

Well, a sailor named McClure tried several times in the same week to apply for a day off and was turned down each time.

So the following week, he entered another request.

"I have an uncle coming into the Baltimore Train Station. He has only one arm and two suitcases, so I want to go help him," McClure wrote as his reason for requesting an off-duty day.

Finally, he received his requested day off.

Chapter 85

Expecting
Our First Child

Towards the end of this tour at Severn River Naval Command, we found out that Mary Lou was pregnant with our first child. The due date was calculated to be in January of 1955. Sure enough, James William Gibson II, nicknamed "Bill," was born on January 2.

Also about this same time, I received orders to report to the submarine *USS Carbonero* (SS-337), home ported in Port Hueneme, located on the West Coast about 120 miles north of Los Angeles.

So we packed up our things and loaded Mary Lou and our new baby boy into the car for a drive to my folks' place in Mount Jackson for a short visit as they had not yet seen little Bill.

I continued across country by car to Port Hueneme while Mary Lou and Bill later traveled by airplane from Pittsburgh to San Francisco. They would stay at her parent's home in nearby Vallejo until I got settled in at my new duty station.

In a few weeks, Mary Lou and Bill arrived in Port Hueneme where we resided until 1956.

Port Hueneme is home to the Naval Construction Battalions or Seabees.

At Port Hueneme, there were three submarines moored alongside the *USS Norton Sound* (AVM-1) in the port area: *USS Tunny*

(SSG-282), *USS Carbonero* (SSG-337) and *USS Cusk* (SSG-348) made up this division of missile testing submarines.

This group or division was one of the first of several submarine divisions to commence work with guided missiles in or on a submarine platform. They started with the old Loon, which was a spin-off of the German World War II buzz bombs.

During my time at Port Hueneme, the systems were upgraded to the Regulus 1 standard for a subsonic missile system. The Regulus missile system, when installed, was designed to place a large pod containing the missile on the *Tunny*'s topside deck.

The *Tunny* would carry a missile concealed in the pod to a predetermined distance from a target, open up the pod and launch the missile. The other two submarines would position themselves much further ahead along the missile's intended trajectory and would guide it in to its intended target.

Of course, we practiced this with dummy war heads and only while very far out at sea to keep prying eyes away as well as for operational safety reasons.

Chapter 86

A Goal Worth Chasing

My duties on board the *USS Carbonero* once again placed me in charge of the Forward Engine Room. This was quite a promotion and an increase in responsibility. I was there now not only to operate and work on the two engines but to supervise the maintenance and repair of the engines and other equipment in the compartment.

I had responsibility for five other Enginemen serving under me to assist in those duties.

Also, I was now back on submarine duty pay and that was a good thing since Mary Lou and I had decided that she would be a stay-at-home Mom until our family was raised.

One night, while on board serving in-port security duty, I had the 1200 to 0400 watch below decks.

During one of my walking inspection tours throughout the boat and into the Forward Battery Compartment where the officers' staterooms were located, I saw an officer's hat.

Partly out of curiosity but mostly from envy, I placed the hat on my own head.

At that moment, I promised myself and my family that someday I would become a Navy officer. From that time on, I pointed my career towards that goal.

Chapter 87

Stay or Play

While serving on the *USS Carbonero*, whenever I was off-duty and in port, I played baseball for the base team named the Seabees. This pastime eventually caused me to make a very large decision that affected my family and me for the rest of our lives.

As a team, the Seabees were so good that we were selected to tour the United States for two months and play other Navy teams throughout the country. The team manager wanted me to accompany the team as a pitcher.

One day, the Seabees manager came down to the boat and asked my Captain if I could go on tour with the team.

The Captain called me up to his stateroom and, after some discussion regarding the team tour, he put me on the spot.

"Do you want to be an officer or do you want to be a jock and remain an Engineman First Class for the rest of your Navy career?" he asked point blank

Oh, how I wanted to go on that baseball tour with the team!

However, I told the Captain that my decision was to stay on the boat and prepare for a commission.

As fun as that baseball team tour might have been, to this day I believe I made the right choice.

Chapter 88

War Story

"Of all the branches of men in the forces, there is none which shows more devotion and faces grimmer perils than the submariners."
Sir Winston Churchill

About a year after I joined the *Carbonero* crew, the ship was deemed ready for a major shipyard overhaul. Mare Island Naval Shipyard was selected as the repair yard.

This was familiar territory for me and our family.

As the *Carbonero* worked her way up the West coast towards the shipyard, our crew was conducting onboard training all the way.

Once again, the family traveled to Vallejo to be with me and stayed with Mary Lou's folks in Vallejo, close to Mare Island.

While on the *Carbonero*, I had the honor of serving with the late Chief Petty Officer Paul Saunders. He had most famously served as a crew member aboard the *USS Barb* (SS-220) during World War II.

For more of his war-time adventures, I advise a reading of *Thunder Below* by Rear Admiral Eugene Fluckey.

In that book, Paul Saunders was named as one of the *Barb*'s shore party assigned to blow up a key railroad bridge used by the enemy to transport men, ammunition, supplies, tanks, trucks and jeeps.

Because of the crew's skill and attention to detail, a heavily laden enemy troop train was crossing the ill-fated bridge at the very same moment the *Barb*'s shore party blew up the bridge.

Chapter 89

Jumping Ship

While waiting for the *Carbonero*'s repairs to complete, I received orders to transfer to the *USS Rock* (SSR-274), also being overhauled at Mare Island.

USS Rock (SSR-274) at launch   US Navy Photo

The *Rock* was one of 28 submarines built in Manitowoc, Wisconsin, during World War II.

Unlike the practice at most other shipyards, the Manitowoc boats were launched sideways instead of stern first.

The *USS Rock* was home-ported in San Diego and scheduled to go to the Western Pacific or WestPac for an extended deployment.

With my new orders, Mary Lou and I decided that she and our son Bill should stay in Vallejo with her parents as she was now expecting our second child.

Whenever possible, I promised to see my growing family, even if it meant I had to hitch hike.

Our second child, Richard Kevin Gibson, was born while I was aboard the *USS Rock* and deployed in the Western Pacific.

Chapter 90

Bugler's Call

"Submariners are a bunch of intelligent misfits that somehow seem to get along, understand each other and work well together."

Unknown
Submitted by "Grump" Barrie
MMCM (SS)

Most submarines during the 1950s still had men onboard who served in submarines during World War II. Some of these sailors were sure enough characters. One such character aboard the *USS Rock* was Fred Dickmeyer.

Fred was part of the crew that had put the *USS Peto* (SS-282) in commission and made nine war patrols on her during World War II. That wasn't a record, but that certainly was a lot of time under stress and avoiding lots of depth charges hurled from Japanese anti-submarine ships and enemy aircraft.

Prior to the *USS Rock*'s departure for peacetime deployment to WestPac, an order came down from the Captain that each and every enlisted man onboard would have to complete a Navy correspondence course during our six-month cruise.

Most of us decided on a course that would help us advance in our ratings or specialties.

Fred was not interested in advancement or in taking any correspondence course, required or not. He had some financial interests that allowed him to be very independent.

The boat's education and information officer, Lieutenant Don White, was responsible for getting the course descriptions out to the crew.

When he asked Dickmeyer what course he wanted, Fred responded, "I don't want any course."

Well, Fred and Lt. White went round and round with Lt. White standing in the Control Room yelling at Fred, who was down in the Pump Room, a compartment one level below the Control Room.

After a couple of exchanges, however, Fred acquiesced and asked for a bugler's course.

"A what?" yelled Lt. White.

"Yes! A bugler's course," Fred replied.

A day or so later, Lt. White received the course and gave it to Fred.

"Where's my bugle?" Fred promptly asked.

"Your what?" Lt. White responded.

"I must have a bugle to practice with so I can complete my bugler's course," Fred replied.

From some unknown source, Lt. White eventually procured Fred a bugle just before the *USS Rock* got underway for WestPac.

On our first night out at sea, somewhere around 2 a.m., there was an awful racket coming up from the Pump Room. The Commanding Officer, who slept in the after end of the Forward Battery Compartment next to the Pump Room, was startled out of a deep sleep and stepped blurry-eyed into the Control Room.

"What in the hell was all that racket?" he demanded gruffly.

"That's Dickmeyer, sir. He's just practicing his correspondence course, sir!" The Chief of the Watch answered with a sly grin.

"Well, tell him to keep that noise down," the Captain told the Chief.

About an hour later, Fred starts in again to practice his bugle.

A couple of minutes later, here comes Lt. White bursting into the Control Room. He had also been blasted out of a sound sleep.

"Give me the *%^$#@ bugle!" Lt. White called down to Fred, who was blatting away in the Pump Room.

"I can't. I have to practice," Fred answered.

"Give me the bugle!" Lt. White responded.

"Sign my course," Fred replied.

So Lt. White signed Fred's correspondence course as "faithfully completed" and recovered the offending bugle.

To the best of my knowledge, the *USS Rock* was and remains for all of history to be the one and only United States submarine to have a qualified bugler on board.

As a matter of further interest, we also had a relatively famous officer come on board the *Rock*.

He was Lieutenant Junior Grade Pete Blair. He was a premier world-class heavyweight wrestler at the US Navy Academy and earlier, during the 1956 summer Olympics, Blair had won a bronze medal.

One of the *Rock*'s more notorious Chief Petty Officers was named Dennis.

Dennis was an old salt and never shined his shoes. In fact, much of the time his shoes were oil-soaked and very dull looking.

One day, several of us came back early from beach liberty and one of us had the bright idea to shine one of Dennis' shoes.

This took a lot of effort, but after a while that shoe really began to glisten. We carefully placed it back under his bunk, right beside its unshined mate.

The next morning our entire crew was mustered topside for a body count to determine whether we needed to send the Shore Patrol out for any missing sailors.

Chief Dennis was nowhere to be seen, however.

Once dismissed, each coconspirator found a reason to pass by the Chief Petty Officer's area where Dennis was busy checking all of the spare shoes to find his other dull one.

Chapter 91

On the Picket Line

In 1956, while the *Rock* was in the Western Pacific, a US Navy surveillance airplane crashed near the China mainland, just inside the three-mile territorial limit.

The airplane was carrying some very sensitive equipment, so the Seventh Fleet sent several ships into the area to retrieve the downed plane.

This was done despite some very strong protests from the Chinese government and military.

For the Seventh Fleet to safely do this, they had to constantly fly an air guard over that area to protect the fleet's surface ships.

Since the *Rock* was a radar picket submarine with some of the latest radar and communications equipment installed during its retrofitting at Mare Island, the *Rock* was required to guide and direct the Air Cap guard and patrol planes watching over the Seventh Fleet's ships.

As a result, the *Rock* was anchored on the surface just outside the three-mile territorial limit of the Chinese coast for 21 days.

As a matter of added security, every hatch opening from the inside to the outside was secured and chained down.

The only entry or exit to the submarine was through the upper conning tower hatch.

For this very important duty, the *USS Rock* and its crew received the China Service Medal.

This extended tour also meant I spent a very long time away from home, my expectant wife Mary Lou and our first son Bill.

Chapter 92

Mixing Oil and Sea Water

While returning from the China Incident, one of *Rock*'s main engines in the Forward Engine Room was almost totally destroyed and thought to be unrepairable by shipboard personnel or any other repair services available afloat.

Apparently, the person on watch was not alert and the lubricating oil sump or storage tank gained 300 gallons of sea water in a short period of time.

The heat exchanger, a lubicating oil cooler on that class of submarine, used sea water to cool the engine oil. Unaware the lube cooler had ruptured, the engine room watch had allowed sea water to enter the lube oil's closed system.

The contaminated lube oil then passed through the primary main engine. When sea water mixes with lubricating oil, the oil loses any of its lubricating qualities and allows metal to metal contact. This destroyed the engine's crankshaft and any associated bearings.

This was a terrible engine casualty that caused a lot of extra work for the entire crew, but especially for us engine men.

The *Rock* was ordered to moor alongside a large repair ship, the *USS Ajax* (AR-6), in Sasebo, Japan. After several conferences, a new crankshaft for that type of engine was located at Mare Island Naval Shipyard.

It was decided that the ship's company, along with the repair ship's assistance and a small repair facility in Sasebo, would remove the damaged crankshaft and install a new one.

As best we knew, this operation had never before been attempted, let alone successfully accomplished, outside of a land-based shipyard.

Chapter 93

Engine Repair

To complete this particular repair, we had to remove much of the major machinery in both engine rooms and place large pieces in other sections of the *Rock* or store them topside.

This evolution took us 28 days and nights of solid work.

Just to give you an idea of the scope of this job, the old crankshaft had to be removed through the after engine room hatch, a large opening to topside, and the new one brought down through that same hatch opening.

To add to this, an auxiliary engine and generator located in the after engine room directly under the access hatch was wedged between the number three and number four main engines. It also had to be unbolted and moved 29 inches to the port or left side.

That was no small task in itself.

In the forward engine room, piping from both of the very large air compressors had to be dismantled and that piping stored in the forward torpedo room at the very bow or front of the submarine.

It order to loosen the crankshaft, the affected main engine had to be totally disassembled and loosened from its bed plates. It then had to be leaned way over to the starboard or right side of the engine room while the crankshaft was unbolted and removed.

But that could only be done after each and every lower part of the engine was also disassembled.

As we were rigging the old crankshaft out of the forward engine-room, it had to be moved into the After Engine Room where we could stand it on end and lift it out of the submarine. The new crankshaft then had to be lowered into the same small opening and moved into the forward engine room.

Then it was finally ready to be installed.

When stood on end, each of the crankshafts cleared the engine-room bilges or hull by just three-eighths of an inch.

Once the new crankshaft was in place, the disassembly process was reversed and all systems had to be restored to their normal operating condition.

Only at this time could the main engine be determined to be in full operating condition.

During this entire 28-day-and-night process, I and a shipmate — my close friend Joe Knox — did not leave the boat until the replacement procedure was complete.

Chapter 94

Just Desserts

When we were finished and the repaired engine was running like new, the Chief Petty Officer in charge told Joe and me to go ashore with expressed orders that he did not want to see us for two full days.

Well, we sequestered ourselves in a bar/hotel and enjoyed quite a few adult beverages before returning to the boat. During this period of 1956-57, the Japanese Maritime Self Defense Force dressed in full uniform to guard the US Navy base entry gates.

As Joe and I were returning to the boat, we passed by one of these guards. This was not that long after the end of World War II and those guards saluted anything American.

Well, as you might surmise, Joe and I were still super hung over. As we approached the main gate of the Sasebo Naval Base, the uniformed guard snapped to attention and saluted as we passed by.

"*Ohio*," the guard politely gave the Japanese phrase for good morning.

Joe never raised his head, but promptly replied, "Cleveland" as we made our way back to the boat. He explained later that during the war, American troops often used state names and cities as security codes when going through checkpoints or returning from behind enemy lines.

Chapter 95

Third Lesson Learned

At the close of our WestPac trip, the *USS Rock* returned to San Diego where I was once again reunited with my family.

But our family of three had grown and now included our number two son, Richard Kevin Gibson, otherwise known as Rich.

A short time later, I was selected to go to Great Lakes, Illinois, to attend Class C of Engineman School. This engine school was on the General Motors Engine 278A that many of the World War II submarines used for their main propulsion.

One of the ancillary subjects in support of this type of engine was the Woodard Governor that controlled the engine's speed.

The governor uses light oil going through different piping systems to regulate the shaft that goes to the engine injectors and controls how much fuel is allowed for the injectors to accept. This is how the governor controls engine speed.

For instructional purposes, a chart illustrating this showed different colored lines indicating the passage of oil flowing through pipes to show how the governor worked.

Being a total wise ass, I raised my hand.

"Do you have a question?" inquired the Chief Petty Officer, a very serious person teaching this part of the class.

"When the engine is running, how do you keep those different colored oils from running together?" I asked innocently.

For my wise-ass remark, I earned a trip to see the officer in charge of the school.

He discussed with me in very strong terms that the school was there for sailors to learn and not for my private amusement.

Chapter 96

Going Nuclear

After graduating from that school and returning to the *USS Rock* and several more months of local operations, I was then selected to attend the Navy's Nuclear Power School in New London, Conn.

All of this happened for my benefit and education because of a fine Engineering Officer and the *Rock*'s Executive Officer. They were always on the lookout for men who they thought had some potential and a future in the up-and-coming nuclear Navy.

The nuclear power school was a six-months assignment, so Mary Lou and the boys were allowed to accompany me at the Navy's expense. We lived first in New London and then in Groton, Conn.

This was a very demanding school for me and required a tremendous amount of study, both in class and even more study after hours.

There were three or four other students at the school and I would invite them all to our house after classes. We would study together until very late each evening.

Mary Lou would usually fix something for all of us to eat after she had fed our two boys.

I wanted to be in the top 10 percent of the class so I could pick my next duty station.

It was my stated desire to further my schooling at the Nuclear Power Training Unit (NPTU) near Arco, Idaho.

I met my goal by eight-hundredths of a percent.

Chapter 97

Making Ends Meet

The Nuclear Power Training program assignment proved to be a very tough time for Mary Lou, who was trying to make ends meet paying bills and feeding our growing family. We had once again lost my submarine duty bonus pay because I was attending classes on shore.

The only family recreation we enjoyed most weekends was on Friday evenings when we would all get into the car, grab a bucket of home-made popcorn and a thermos of Kool-Aid, and head for the $1 a carload drive-in movie theater. The name of the movie did not matter.

Several times since then, Mary Lou has had to make do with as much or less.

During this time, our younger son Rich became very sick with a serious ear and throat infection. It was touch and go with his health for a while.

I must stop here and briefly tell you about our two fine boys.

Both of our sons are now men, ages 62 and 60 respectively. Bill is retired from a career with the California Department of Transportation in their road sign department.

Rich is the manager of two restaurants in the Puget Sound area of Washington State.

Raising our sons and managing our money were Mary Lou's primary duties.

My wife comes from a long line of English relatives. Most of her relations came from the southern part of England called Cornwall, famous for producing underground miners who scattered all over the world chasing the work they loved.

After much training as a machinist, Lou's father Frederick Cecil Buckthought emigrated to the United States in 1923.

He and his first wife passed through Ellis Island, the East coast's port of entry for much of Europe, and settled in Butte, Montana. His first job was not as a machinist, but at 3,500 feet below ground where he worked as a miner digging for copper.

In a relatively short time, mostly because of his wife's poor health, they moved to Grass Valley, California. There he found work as a machinist in the now famous Empire Gold Mine.

After a period of time, his wife passed away.

Later he met and married Myrtle Kent, whose heritage was also English. Myrtle was also a first-generation immigrant from the Cornwall area.

On August 27, 1933, Mary Louise Buckthought was born.

When she 9, her dad found work at Mare Island Naval Shipyard in Vallejo, Calif. Vallejo is an inland port city in Solano County, located 30 miles north of San Francisco on the northeastern shore of San Pablo Bay.

In 1942, when the Buckthought family moved there, Vallejo was a Navy town and home of the bustling Mare Island Naval Shipyard where submarines were built, modified or repairs made for service in World War II.

After graduating from Vallejo High School, Mary Lou also found work at Mare Island as a supply clerk.

Mary Lou spent 22 years of our married life with me in the Navy. For 11 of those 22 years, I was away from home quite a lot.

Hence, she raised our two sons to be the fine men they are today, and she did all of this on a shoe-string budget.

Navy paychecks then were nothing like what sailors receive today.

Whenever I needed help, I knew she was a ready and able assistant on whom I could count, whether that meant typing ship board orders, maintaining a pleasant home environment, or later in my career, being a great hostess when we entertained.

Chapter 98

Hunter's Paradise

When our younger son Richard finally recovered, I was completing the Navy's Nuclear Power School. I was then transferred to the Naval Nuclear Power Unit (NPTU) in Arco, Idaho, first as a student and later as an instructor.

Because Richard's health was still frail, Mary Lou and our two boys returned once again to Vallejo to stay with her folks.

During this time I completed my studies and, in turn, was qualified as a reactor operator with orders to remain in Arco as a full-time reactor operator and instructor.

Mary Lou and the boys then rejoined me and we moved into a nice little apartment in Blackfoot, Idaho. A couple months later we moved to a more spacious house in nearby Idaho Falls.

This was an enjoyable place to live and my schedule allowed us plenty of free weekends to explore that area of the country even though I worked many hours during the week at the training school, both as an operator and with a lot of advanced study.

Yet again, we were without submarine pay and our menus were limited. However, we ate well and survived pleasantly.

As mentioned, the hunting and fishing in that eastern part of Idaho was sensational. I did way too much of both those activities during my off-duty hours. As a result, the time I did spend with Mary Lou and the boys suffered, much to my later regret.

However, Mary Lou's skillful planning and budget management — along with the elk that we shot and the trout I caught — surely helped supply our dinner table with excellent fare that year.

As a family, we were also able to do quite a bit of touring and camping.

I fixed up an old 1949 GMC panel truck with four beds in it. This allowed us to spend several wonderful weekends camping in and touring through nearby Yellowstone National Park.

We also used the truck to visit other camping areas. but Yellowstone was our favorite with plenty of bears to see.

Chapter 99

Instructing Legends

"Great minds discuss ideas, average minds discuss events, small minds discuss people."
Admiral Hyman G. Rickover

Later that same year, I was selected to be a mechanical instructor for prospective commanding officers of nuclear submarines.

Among the officers I was instructing, three of them would go on to become admirals.

The first of these was Commander Robert Lyman John Long, who went on to reach the rank of a four-star admiral.

Long served as Vice Chief of Naval Operations from 1977 to 1979 and Commander in Chief of the Pacific from 1979 to 1983.

Long graduated from the US Naval Academy in 1943, served on the battleship *USS Colorado* in the Pacific and entered submarine service after World War II.

Admiral Robert L.J. Long

He saw combat in the Vietnam War and commanded the *USS Sea Leopard*, a diesel-powered submarine; the *USS Patrick Henry* and the *USS Casimir Pulaski*, both of which were nuclear-powered ballistic missile submarines.

Long also commanded the Submarine Force, United States Atlantic fleet; Submarines, Allied Command; and Submarine Force, Western Atlantic area.

The second of my most distinguished students was Commander Oliver "Hap" Hazard Perry, Jr., who retired as a Vice-Admiral in 1975 after 33 years in the Navy. He died in 2003.

The son of a Tennessee sheriff, Hap Perry was the namesake of Oliver Hazard Perry, a Naval hero during the War of 1812.

A 1943 graduate of the US Naval Academy at Annapolis, Md., Hap Perry served as a Chief Gunnery Officer on board the destroyer *USS Mullany* (DD-528) during the latter part of World War II.

Off Okinawa late in 1944, the *Mullany* was attacked by at least four Japanese kamikazes led by Takeichi Minoshima, pilot of a Nakajima Ki-43 fighter, a plane known to Americans as an Oscar.

All four enemy planes were fired upon but one, flown by Minoshima, crashed into the Mullany killing 21 American sailors, wounding 36 more and causing nine to go missing.

The Mullany, with Hap Perry aboard, eventually limped into San Francisco with only its starboard engine in commission.

During an extensive dry-dock period for repairs, Hap Perry took some time to get married to Joan Thomson of Los Angeles and re-enlisted, but this time volunteering for service on board the Navy's diesel-powered submarines.

Hap and Joan enjoyed 58 years of marriage and raised two sons, Oliver Perry III and William Perry.

Perry went on to a distinguished Navy career. He rose to command the world's most powerful nuclear submarines, the Polaris-armed *USS Theodore Roosevelt* (SSBN-600) and *USS Sam Rayburn* (SSBN-635), as well as all NATO undersea forces in the Mediterranean.

When Perry retired, he had three stars on his shoulder boards and wore a chestful of campaign ribbons and decorations including a Bronze Star and a Distinguished Service Medal.

The last of the three up-and-coming officers that I had the privilege to teach was Commander Paul L. Lacy, Jr., who was promoted to Rear Admiral in July 1967.

We became close friends when he became my boss as Commander, Submarine Force, US Pacific Fleet from 1970-72.

Rear Admiral Paul L. Lacy Jr.

Early on in his career, Lacy was a representative on the battleship *USS Missouri* (BB-63) during the signing of Japanese surrender documents on Sept. 2, 1945. He went on to command two diesel-powered submarines, the *USS Guitarro* (SS-363) and the *USS Pickerel* (SS-524), prior to being selected for the Navy's first group of commanding officers of fleet ballistic missile nuclear submarines. He commanded the Blue Crew of the Polaris-armed submarine *USS Ethan Allen* (SSBN-608).

Lacy was promoted to Rear Admiral in July 1967. He retired from the Navy in March 1973. Among his medals and awards are the Distinguished Service Medal, the Legion of Merit with Combat V and Gold Star, the Navy Commendation Medal with Gold Star, and the Navy Unit Commendation Medal with Gold Star.

After retirement from the Navy, Lacy continued to serve the public in the Hawaii State Constitutional Convention in 1978 and was elected to serve two terms in the Hawaii State House of Representatives.

Later he helped develop the *USS Bowfin* Museum in Pearl Harbor, dedicated to the Pacific Fleet submariners of World War II.

He died on July 14, 2013, in Cohasset, Mass.

He was buried next to his late wife, Katherine M. Kerley, at the National Memorial Cemetery of the Pacific in Honolulu, Hawaii.

Chapter 100

Going AWOL

Staff and students alike worked for the now famous Admiral Hyman G. Rickover, widely acknowledged as Father of the Nuclear Navy at the Nuclear Power Unit in Arco, Idaho. Rickover's primary responsibility was nuclear reactor safety, not the tactics or strategies for wartime submarine operations.

Rickover was known for his strictness.

He had a standing order that prospective commanding officers in training could not leave the Naval Nuclear Power Unit training center site during the entire six weeks they were assigned to the school.

He believed that they were out there for a

Admiral Hyman G. Rickover

reason and supposed to spend all of their spare time studying.

Rickover was always demanding of others, had little tolerance for mediocrity and could not abide stupidity.

Nevertheless, Rickover's military authority and mandate from Congress were absolute with regard to the US fleet's reactor operations. To those of us who worked for him, he was a god-like presence and ruled with an iron hand.

It was also required that I work closely with the aforementioned three fine officers destined for later greatness.

After a couple of weeks, my high-ranking students politely let me know that they were not going to be "all the way out there in eastern Idaho" for any extended period of time without seeing at least some of the surrounding countryside.

I offered to help if I could, so we devised a covert plan to got them off the training site in the back of my car.

One morning, I drove out of the Arco training site with one officer lying down in the trunk of my car. The other two officers were lying down in the car's back seat, covered over with a blanket.

We spent an entire day driving throughout southern Idaho. About noon we were growing hungry, so I telephoned Mary Lou and asked her to fix some lunch for our foursome.

You can imagine her nervousness at having three Commanders arriving at our house for brunch. Back then, however, she was even nervous around Chief Petty Officers.

We all had a great time on our secret outing and I was successful in sneaking the three Commanders back onto the training site at the end of their excursion with no one being the wiser.

Chapter 101

Witty Repartee

One of the many official visitors to the Nuclear Power Unit training site was an officer who I will not name other than to describe him as a wonderful person and a perfect gentleman.

Everyone liked this man because he never swore and did not much appreciate those who did.

During his visit, he and several other officers were in a café in Idaho Falls having breakfast. When they were finished, this gentleman wanted to pay his very small tab with a $20 bill.

When the waitress brought back his change, she handed him 18 silver dollars. These were the days of hard money in Idaho and silver dollars were often used as change.

This prompted the officer to gently reprimand the young woman.

"If I put all of these silver dollars in my pocket, it will put my pants down," he said.

"If you give them to me, I will pull my pants down," the waitress replied with an impish grin.

Before that moment, I do not believe that I had ever seen a gentleman blush that particular color.

Chapter 102

Jumping Ladders

"A ship in port is safe; but that is not what ships are built for. Sail out to sea and do new things!"
Rear Admiral Grace Brewster Murray Hopper
Computer scientist, US Navy

During the period from 1953 to 1960, it was almost impossible for an enlisted man to advance to the rank of Chief Petty Officer in my chosen field as Engineman.

Therefore, I decided to stake my chances at becoming a Warrant Officer. As fate would have it, about that same time the Navy brass decided to cancel the Warrant Officer program.

As a lucky result, I was simultaneously selected to become an Ensign, Limited Duty Officer.

That was a very difficult decision for me because the rank of Chief Petty Officer was at the top of the enlisted ranks advancement ladder with all of the pay benefits that ensue.

Meanwhile, the Ensign rank of Limited Duty Officer was at the bottom of a ladder leading up to the commissioned officer ranks.

I consulted with my three co-conspirators, the three prospective commanding officer trainees temporarily under my care and instruction.

Each of them advised me never to turn down an advancement.

Their collective advice was to get my tail back to sea where I could learn be a proper Navy officer.

That was one proud day for me when I finally put on the single gold stripe and became an Ensign in the US Navy.

That change in status and rank started me on a new career.

Chapter 103

Starting Over

"Helm, Bridge. What are you doing 60 degrees off course?"
"Bridge, Helm. Coming back from 90 degrees, sir."
Unknown
Submitted by Roger Forgit
USS Tigrone (AGSS-419)

We stayed on in Idaho for a couple more months. During that time, I was assigned as Assistant Training Officer at the submarine unit and worked for a less than extremely talented Lieutenant.

One day, the Lieutenant was serving as Officer on Watch in the reactor maneuvering room from where the reactor was controlled. The reactor was up and running and low and behold, the person standing behind the Lieutenant on watch was none other than the kind old gentleman Admiral Hyman G. Rickover, well known for suffering no fools.

About this time, the Lieutenant called into the engine-room to the petty officer on watch.

"Start Number One. 1C-MG set," the Lieutenant commanded.

"I can't!" the petty officer responded.

"Don't argue with me! I said start Number One. 1C-MG set," the Lieutenant barked back.

To which the petty officer give the militarily correct reply to any direct order.

"Aye, aye, sir!" he said.

All of a sudden, the reactor shut down. Then, just as suddenly, it restarted.

This caused the Lieutenant and others, including Admiral Rickover, to rush from the control room into the engine room.

"What happened?" the Lieutenant angrily demanded.

"I started Number One. 1C-MG set, sir!" the petty officer calmly replied.

"But I had to stop it first because it was already running," he explained with a wide grin.

Well, that Lieutenant was going to be wiping egg off his own face for quite some time after.

Chapter 104

Survivor's Remorse

*"Since human wisdom cannot secure us from accidents,
it is the greatest effort of reason to bear them well."*
John Paul Jones
Naval Commander
American Revolutionary War

Serving with me for a time at the Nuclear Power Training Unit in Arco, Idaho, was Ray McCool, a former submarine shipmate of mine when we were both aboard the *USS Conger* in1949.

Ray was a very fine sailor. He was also one of the best looking men I ever saw in that era including many of Hollywood's leading movie stars. In fact, Ray could almost pass as a double for Robert Wagner.

By the time I met up with Ray in Idaho, he was an officer as well as an instructor. Following his stint with me in Idaho, Ray was ordered to serve in the commissioning crew of the nuclear-powered attack submarine *USS Thresher* (SSN-593) in Portsmouth, New Hampshire.

Most people may remember that the *Thresher* suffered a terrible disaster while conducting sea trials and was lost with all hands on April 10, 1963.

Ray was scheduled to go out with the boat on those sea trials, but that same morning he received a call from the Portsmouth Naval

Hospital that his wife had been badly burned in a kitchen grease fire.

Over Ray's sincere objections, the *Thresher*'s Commanding Officer ordered Ray to stay on shore and tend to his wife and family.

Until the day he died, however, Ray never did overcome the survivor's guilt and grief he suffered as a result of not being with his shipmates on that ill-fated submarine.

Chapter 105

Officer and Gentleman

"Like the destroyer, the submarine has created its own type of officer and man with language and traditions apart from the rest of the service, and yet at the heart unchangingly of the service."

Author **Rudyard Kipling**
The Fringes of the Fleet, 1915

While at Arco, I was ordered to report to Limited Duty Officer's School in Newport, Rhode Island.

This school was also known as the Knife and Fork School. It was designed to help newly appointed officers convert from enlisted status to their new role as a commissioned officer.

During this training period, Mary Lou and the boys traveled to Mount Jackson, Penn., where they enjoyed a great visit with my parents.

Before leaving Idaho, I was also advised that I would be assigned to the *USS Pomfret* (SS-391), home ported in San Diego, once I successfully completed the Limited Duty Officer training program.

As it turned out, I was one of just three submarine Limited Duty Officers in my year group to be returned to diesel submarines for active duty on board.

Once my Limited Duty Officer training was completed, the family and I left Mount Jackson together and motored across the country to arrive in San Diego during the fall of 1960.

Already familiar with San Diego from an earlier duty assignment there, we quickly settled into a rented home on Childs Avenue nearby Chula Vista.

We lived there for approximately five months until we were finally able to purchase a home in the San Diego subdivision of Allied Gardens.

Chapter 106

Qualifying
as an Officer

I reported on board the *USS Pomfret* (SS-391), in December of 1960.

The Commanding Officer, Lieutenant Commander Jerry Nuss, was a great guy. He was very demanding. He told me my first and primary duty was to qualify as an officer in submarines.

This was to be a nine-month intensive study along with a detailed notebook.

The qualification process includes drawing and memorizing each and every system on board the submarine, as well as a working knowledge of what each system does.

This includes knowing the theory behind each system and why a system or an electrical circuit performs as it is designed to do.

Additionally, I had to accomplish this while also serving as a division officer and qualifying as an Officer of the Deck, both while under way and in port.

I was officially given the position of Assistant Engineering Officer and was given charge of the boat's electrical division personnel, so I set about mapping the boat's extensive electrical system.

A few months later, I was promoted to head up the submarine's supply department while still qualifying for officer status on board a submarine. This gave me a thorough knowledge of the boat's supply capabilities and the use of each item on board.

I did have one advantage over other commissioned officers in that I had already qualified for submarines during my time as an enlisted man. From that experience, I knew and had already worked with most of a submarine's mechanical and electrical systems.

At the same time, I also had to qualify as an in-port Duty Officer and Officer of the Deck while underway.

The Duty Officer is responsible for what happens in and on the boat while it is in port. That is especially true whenever the Captain and other officers are ashore.

The Officer of the Deck underway has responsibility for the submarine when she is at sea and reports directly to the Captain.

Learning about all of these duties was more than a full plate.

Chapter 107

Guide to
Pink Elephants

The *USS Pomfret*'s Executive Officer at that time was Lieutenant Commander Barney Barnette, another great officer who was a lot of help to me. One day, Barnette called me into his state room and informed me that along with all these other responsibilities I would be the SLJO for the wardroom.

"What does that entail?" I asked curiously.

"You will find out soon enough!" was his response.

Later I asked another officer and found out the acronym stood for Shitty Little Jobs Officer.

Barnette was surely right. I took care of everything from getting plaques for different events to taking inventory of all of the onboard drugs and medicinal alcohol.

Being SLJO had its fun times as well. The Captain felt very strongly that our wardroom should participate in Squadron activities and make the name of our ship and its crew known socially.

The Squadron Three submarines and their respective staff members were scheduled to have a Thanksgiving Day party at the Admiral Baker Officers Club and the *USS Pomfret* wardroom was invited.

It was Mary Lou's and my turn to have our wardroom officers over to our home for a pre-party function. I did not want to spend the better part of my time at our house mixing alcoholic drinks, so I decided to serve a punch with some kick.

On the afternoon of the party, I took out my handy *"Guide to Pink Elephants"* recipe book and found one entry for Artillery Punch that looked promising.

The directions appeared to be very straight forward. It talked about bourbon rum and vodka.

Please notice that there are no commas in the preceding sentence.

I didn't notice them in the recipe either.

You guessed it. All three types of alcohol went into the punch bowl, along with some fruit juice and some mixer.

Well, we hosted the pre-party all right, then we adjourned to the real party and now we were a part of the entertainment.

For example, one of *Pomfret*'s officers was observed talking animatedly to a wooden post regarding a popular dance step.

The rest of us were not in much better shape.

The next day, back onboard our submarine, the Captain declared that there would be no more pre-parties and that I would observe commas from that time forward.

Chapter 108

Herbert O. Burton

Lieutenant Commander Barnette was shortly relieved as Executive Officer and transferred. The *Pomfret*'s new Executive Officer was Lieutenant Commander Herbert O. Burton.

During the ensuing years, Herb Burton and I were to become beyond the best of friends.

Herb came aboard just about the time the boat was scheduled for deployment to the Western Pacific for six months. This extended trip is known in the submarine force as a WestPac trip.

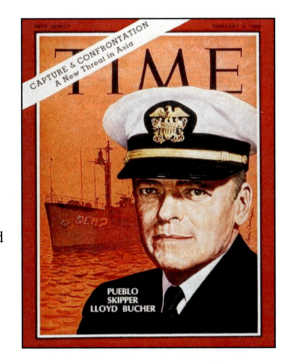

After completing my required notebook and being quizzed and passed by a qualified officer from another submarine — none other than then-Lieutenant Lloyd Mark "Pete" Bucher of the *USS Ronquil* (SS-396).

Later in his career, Bucher was promoted to Commander of the *USS Pueblo* (AGER-2), which was captured on Jan. 23, 1968, by the North Korean Navy.

Now that I had completed the in-port phase of my officer's qualifications, I looked forward to the underway part and finally being a qualified submarine officer.

Every once in a while, usually when I had an idle moment, I would reflect back to 1954 when I was on board the *USS Carbonero* and trying on that officer's hat for the first time.

A lot of water had passed under the keel since then.

During this same period, I was made the ship's supply officer in addition to my other officer qualification duties.

Chapter 109

My Man Finch

"There is a touch of the pirate about every man who wears the dolphins badge."

Commander Jeff Tall
Her Majesty's Royal Navy

As the *USS Pomfret*'s crew was making its final preparations before going to WestPac, the boat was found to have a noisy propeller. This was a significant problem because a noisy propeller is a sure alert on almost any type of underwater listening device.

The sound of a submarine can be tracked and the noise tagged to a particular boat.

As a result, the *Pomfret* was transferred to Hunter's Point Naval Shipyard to change the propeller and repair several smaller items. Hunter's Point is located adjacent to San Francisco.

Upon arriving at Hunter's Point, we moored to a pier next to a very large crane so the bad propeller could be removed and a new one installed. The entire operation lasted about six weeks.

As the supply officer, loading the *Pomfret* for a six-month WestPac deployment was more than a small chore.

The Executive Officer realized this and was soon on the lookout for some assistance for me. As fate would have it, a young sailor reported aboard who had served as supply petty officer on his most recent submarine posting. Thus starts the story of My Man Finch.

Finch was a fine young sailor, but was a little on the slow side mentally.

Well, shortly after Finch joined us, Captain Nuss casually mentioned to me that he would like to have a motion picture projector for the officer's wardroom.

This projector was to be an extra projector as the enlisted men already had one in the crew's mess. The desired second projector would allow the boat's officers to view movies at their own convenience, rather than be limited to joining the crew during scheduled movie showings.

This second projector, however, was against regulations.

At about the same time, the Engineering Officer asked me to obtain and secure several "controlled items" for our forthcoming WestPac trip.

These controlled items were also not officially allowed.

Well, I casually mentioned the projector and "controlled items" list to Finch. Low and behold, a couple of days later, as I was standing topside, here comes a large Navy truck backing down the pier.

More amazing to me, Finch was in the driver's seat.

I did not know it until then, but Finch had a very rare but completely valid Navy driver's license.

More to my surprise and shock, on board the truck was a brand new motion picture projector as well as all of the "controlled items" that the other officers had requested.

I asked Finch how he came by all the "controlled items."

"You don't want to know, sir!" was his terse reply.

"On the contrary, I really do want to know!" I quickly responded.

Well, Finch said he was at the Oakland Naval Supply Center on the other side of San Francisco Bay and had managed to procure the desired items.

Apparently he had befriended several of the ladies working there and pleaded for their sympathy by convincing them that his mean old supply officer would punish him if he could not procure those items right away.

Much later, I found out that the projector came from the wartime supplies section of the Supply Center, an area that was under strict lock and key with a very no-nonsense Marine guard stationed at the entrance.

For several days thereafter, I nervously waited for armed guards to come haul Finch and me away to the brig.

Finally, still feeling guilty, I persuaded Finch to take a trip with me over to the Oakland Naval Supply Center to thank the ladies responsible for our good fortune.

I intended to present them with several boxes of candy. But more than that, I wanted to show them that I wasn't really some overbearing ogre picking on a poor little enlisted man like Finch.

Anyway, the *Pomfret* now had its two movie projectors and Captain Nuss was happy. His officers, me included, could watch movies in the peace and comfort of our own wardroom whenever we wanted.

Fully repaired, we soon departed for our home port of San Diego.

Chapter 110

Diving Solo

"Submarine life most of the time is hours and hours of boredom with intermittent terror thrown in to keep you on your toes!"

Unknown
Submitted by Paul "PEP" Perris

It was nearly time for the *Pomfret* and its crew to head for the Western Pacific fleet and our new posting to the US Navy Base in Yokosuka, Japan, headquarters for WestPac.

We were soon underway and steaming along on the surface on a peaceful Sunday morning and I was serving as Officer of the Deck.

Captain Nuss was very strict on how his officers were to stand their watches. When one of us was on watch, we should have our mind completely on the boat and constantly be thinking ahead on what to do in case of certain serious evolutions such as a fire or a collision with another vessel.

On this day, however, we were sailing along on a beautiful flat sea and the only thing moving around the boat was an occasional flying fish.

Alas, my mind was not on my duties. It wandered back home to my wife and our family.

Every few moments, I would take a quick check, but nothing was going on down in the boat either except for the routine things connected with normal steaming.

I assumed the Captain and the rest of our boat's officers were either sleeping or eating breakfast.

All of a sudden a voice came over the *Pomfret*'s announcement systems.

"Officer of the Deck, this is the Captain. Submerge the Boat!" the loudspeakers barked.

You can imagine my absolute and utter confusion. I was immediately thrust into a mode that was very near panic.

After trying to collect my wits, I signaled the lookouts — the enlisted men standing watch topside — and ordered them to get below decks.

Simultaneously I sounded the diving alarm.

"Dive, dive!" I screamed into the boat's announcing system that transmitted my command throughout the entire submarine.

I jumped down into the conning tower and reported to the Commanding Officer who was standing calmly beside the main periscope.

"Last man down. Hatch secured!" I declared, my voice quavering just a bit from nerves.

"Very well, make your depth 58 feet," the skipper responded,

"Aye, aye, sir!" I answered, then dropped down to the control room to assume the duties of diving officer.

When I looked around, however, I was surprised to see the normally bustling control room was in fact deserted. Somewhat tentatively, I called up to Captain Nuss in the conning tower.

"There is no one down here, sir," I reported

"I do not want your problems. Get this submarine submerged!" he responded gruffly.

After clearing my mind and collecting my thoughts, I physically started going at lightning speed through the many evolutions that several others would normally do in the control room.

I quickly shut valves that should be shut and opened valves that should be open. I then manned the stern planes operating wheel and leveled the submarine off at a depth of 58 feet, which for us was normal periscope depth.

"Fifty-eight feet," I finally reported to the Commanding Officer.

There was a lot more to it than that, of course, but I won't bore you with all the other happenings or other actions.

I was much too busy to be scared until it was all over.

The sailors normally on watch quickly re-entered the control room and the boat continued on its normal submerged operations.

That was the first and only one-man dive of a modern submarine that I have ever known about, before or since.

Chapter 111

Starry, Starry Night

"Uncommon valor was a common virtue!"
Fleet Admiral Chester W. Nimitz
March 17, 1945

One night as the *Pomfret* was nearing the coastline of Japan, it was once again my turn to stand as Officer of the Deck Underway. There I was for the first time in that small black tube of a Conning Tower, located above the Control Room.

Lieutenant Commander Jerry Nuss, our skipper, had just waved the wand over me and declared that I was now qualified to be the Officer of the Deck Submerged.

It was 1201. In civilian parlance, it was one minute after midnight. It was pitch black on the ocean's surface as far as I could ascertain through the periscope and also in my immediate surroundings in the Conning Tower. The lack of light was intentional so that the watch standers could maintain their night vision with eyes fully dilated.

For the first time in my career, I was responsible for the safety of an entire submarine and its crew. This was called the watch and my shift would last four long hours.

Other watch standers with different responsibilities stood throughout the submarine at their respective stations, of course.

But I was the only one who could see through the periscope and determine where we were heading and whether it was a safe distance from other water craft or rocky shorelines.

I stood watch with my eyes glued to the periscope, maintaining constant surveillance of the water's surface. For all I knew, I was surrounded by the entire Pacific Ocean.

I was very nervous even in my confidence. It somehow seemed appropriate for me to be there alone at this time in my career.

The submarine was conducting a routine patrol during a fleet training exercise and all of the ships in the fleet were looking for our submarine. I could scan only a small quadrant of the undulating horizon at any one time, but I was looking for whatever was in our area of the ocean.

Ah! There was a white light. And then there was also a green light.

That meant the others were still looking for us.

It was time for me to call the Captain to come to the Conning Tower and take charge. It was also time for me to sound the Battle Stations alarm.

So ended my first solo watch on a submerged submarine.

Chapter 112

Custom Tailored

Well, the *Pomfret* eventually arrived in WestPac and moored at the Number 1 pier in Yokosuka, Japan. After a routine two-week upkeep to fix any problems that turned up while en route, we departed Yokosuka for a special operation.

These types of "spec ops" are nicely covered in the book *Blind Man's Bluff: The Untold Story Of American Submarine Espionage*, a New York Times bestseller written by Sherry Sontag and Christopher Drew, with contributions by Annette Lawrence Drew.

By this time, I had qualified as an officer of the deck underway.

After six weeks of demanding operations, we returned once again to Yokosuka, Japan, to replenish our onboard supplies and food stuffs.

I had heard from several former WestPac officers that if I was ever to get posted to Yokosuka, I should stock up on custom-tailored dress uniforms made by Mitto, a very famous local tailor.

I am happy to report that Mitto's workmanship was indeed superb.

More than 50 years later, I am still able to wear two of the uniforms that I purchased from Mitto in 1961. Of course, I have had the suits altered a bit.

But I will not reveal where or by how much.

Chapter 113

Ready for Qualification

After a few more days in port for some needed voyage repairs, the *USS Pomfret* departed for Hong Kong, China, for a port visit to show the American flag and offer a bit of liberty for the crew.

After arriving in Hong Kong, I was temporarily transferred to the submarine *USS Bluegill* (SSK-242) to complete my training as Officer of the Deck underway as required for my officer's qualification.

Once on board, the *Bluegill* was ordered to sail to Naha, Okinawa. Acting as Officer of the Deck underway, I caused the submarine to get underway and clear the port of Hong Kong.

It was a difficult but fun time for the two weeks I spent on board the *Bluegill*. The officers and crew treated me as one of their own.

Each day I was required to act as the Officer in Charge of different evolutions and causalities training.

As we approached Okinawa, I assumed the duties of Navigator. We even made land-fall as of the time I had predicted from plotting the boat's speed, ocean currents and weather conditions.

That was a good time for me to be so precise.

I now assumed the duties as Officer of the Deck as we entered the harbor in Naha, Okinawa.

At certain times, Naha harbor can be one of the most treacherous ports in the Pacific Ocean. This time, however, the seas were flat and we were able to ride in on an in-coming tide.

All went well with the approach and *Bluegill* made the harbor entry safely. I then brought the boat alongside the visitor's pier and caused the submarine to be safely moored.

At that point, the Commanding Officer of *Bluegill* declared me ready to be qualified as an officer in submarines.

I then departed Okinawa and returned to the *USS Pomfret,* once again in Yokosuka.

Chapter 114

Dolphins Get Wet Again

"Submariners are a special brotherhood. Either all come to the surface or no one does. On a submarine, the phrase 'all for one and one for all' is not just a slogan, but reality."
Vice Admiral Rudolf Golvson
Russian Navy

Now that I was fully qualified as an officer and back aboard the *Pomfret*, I received my gold officer dolphins pin with Captain Nuss conducting the ceremony.

I proudly wore my gold officer's dolphins on my uniform along with the silver dolphins that I had earned when I first qualified for submarines as an enlisted man.

Following a long submarine tradition, several of the crew members threw me over the side to wet my gold dolphins.

After my dunking, I went to my stateroom and put on a fresh uniform.

Later that same day, Executive

Qualified for command

Officer Herb Burton called me to his stateroom for a meeting. Burton informed me that I had six weeks in which to present the Commanding Officer with my topic for a thesis.

This would lead to my qualification for eventual command of a diesel submarine.

Burton told me the thesis would entail a six-month to nine-month period of heavy study that I would need to complete along with all of my other assigned duties.

I chose as my topic the *Evasion Tactics for a Diesel Submarine in a War-Time Scenario*, and I completed my thesis in just six weeks of study and research.

After submitting my thesis to the Commanding Officer for approval, I was then quizzed by several senior officers as well as the Division Commander, both while in port and later at sea.

Upon their approval, I was eventually awarded the prestigious designation that qualified me for command of a diesel submarine.

I was now one of the US Navy's very few Limited Duty Officers, and the first Lieutenant Junior Grade to be so qualified for command.

Our six months in WestPac was rapidly drawing to a close and all of us on board the *Pomfret* were looking forward to returning to San Diego and our respective families.

During this intense time of qualifying, I had little opportunity to myself in which to even think about my family, although I knew they were adjusting to life in our own home in San Diego.

Chapter 115

Through Sickness and Health

It was also about this same time frame that I assumed the duty as head of *Pomfret*'s torpedo and gunnery department.

This was no small chore in itself.

All of this study and qualification were tough on me because I had a solid, but limited high school education. Luckily, I did have several very advanced Navy schools under my belt, including the prestigious Navy Nuclear Power Unit experience.

However, I did not have a good background in what you would call the humanities or English composition. If there is any doubt, all one had to do was ask my Executive Officer Herb Burton.

But I did have a very good working knowledge of the machinery and systems inside a diesel submarine.

In addition, I had a wonderful wife and understanding family who supported me in all of my undertakings. Even today, they are all still very supportive.

Yes, I do admit to being gone a lot of the time. Even when the boat was in port, I was usually either working or standing watch as the in port duty officer. Once again, this is when my wife Mary Lou showed her true colors and dedication.

Other than a father's attention, our sons did not lack for anything that she could provide. This certainly was done with a limited and sometimes meager income. Mary Lou took on raising our boys as her full-time job. If she wasn't driving them somewhere to an activity or music lessons, she was at home baking cookies for them or helping them with their homework.

Many evenings and weekends, she would attend school programs, help with Cub Scout or Boy Scout projects, or arrange for piano or guitar lessons. Regularly, she would take the boys and a few of their classmates on school field trips or beach outings with help from some of the other crew spouses.

She was also there when the boys were sick or needed a doctor's expertise with a sprained ankle.

The boys and I both knew we could count on Lou to be a full-time mother and wife. In addition, she also supported me by completing many secretarial duties as my career continued to advance.

Chapter 116

Crown of Thorns

Back aboard the *USS Coucal*, I was shaken from my reveries to tackle the tasks at hand.

In the spring of 1970, the Pacific Ocean around several of the Hawaiian Islands suffered from an infestation of a certain type of starfish that was eating and destroying coral.

The Kalohi Channel off the western side of Molokai was one of the areas to be saved from the so-called Crown of Thorns starfish.

Deep sea divers from the *Coucal*, along with civilian and military scuba divers from throughout the nearby area, were directed to that channel. Our ship stood at anchor for several weeks in support of those divers.

The *Coucal* was an integral part of this mission because we had on board a diving decompression chamber that we could use in case one of the divers might have a diving accident or develop the bends, also known as decompression sickness or Caisson disease.

The bends can occur in scuba divers, deep sea divers or even at high altitudes in some aerospace events when dissolved gases, mainly nitrogen or helium, come out of solution in bubbles and can affect just about any body area including joints, lung, heart, skin and brain.

In commercial as well as Navy deep diving, decompression sickness is experienced by divers who breathe heliox, a special mixture of oxygen and helium.

Nitrogen, helium or any gas from a diver's air tank increases in pressure as a diver descends. For every 33 feet in ocean water, the pressure due to nitrogen goes up another 11.6 pounds per square inch. As the pressure due to nitrogen increases, more nitrogen dissolves into the tissues. Also, the longer a diver remains at depth, the more nitrogen dissolves.

Unlike the oxygen in a compressed air tank that a deep diver uses to work or swim underwater, the nitrogen gas is not utilized by the body and builds up over time in body tissues.

The underlying cause of symptoms throughout the body is due mainly to nitrogen bubbles being released when the diver returns to sea level.

Much like the bubbles that form when carbonated soda is poured into a glass. Carbon dioxide gas molecules dissolved in the solution while under pressure are released and the gas leaves the solution in the form of bubbles.

Similarly, nitrogen bubbles in blood vessels, muscle tissue and various organs of the body expand and block blood flow. In extreme cases, these bubbles can build up in muscle tissue and nerve areas by stretching and tearing them.

The bends can be extremely painful, and in rare cases, can even cause death.

As was now expected, the crew and mechanical operations of the *Coucal* performed in an outstanding manner.

With the *Coucal*'s on-board decompression chamber and careful adherence to diving tables that pre-calculate the amount of time a diver can remain under water as well as how slowly those same divers need to return to the surface, we were able to minimize any problems and address those health issues in our divers before they became seriously affected.

For these services, the *Coucal* and its crew received a formal commendation from the state of Hawaii. This operation was entitled The Crown of Thorns Project.

This was not only a serious task but also a fun one, with plenty of liberty for the remainder of the ship's crew on the nearby island of Molokai.

Chapter 117

Scourge of
the Sea Bat

As is the case in almost every situation, there is a person who is either overly serious or one who wears his rank on his sleeve.

During the Crown of Thorns Project, a Marine Captain was a frequent visitor on board the *Coucal* as he was also a diver who fit the above description.

Not to be taken aback, our Chief Petty Officer Kerr was more than up to putting this person in his place, but in a fun way.

The Chief directed one of our sailors to go up to the chief's quarters and get the "Sea Bat" and bring it and its cage to the fantail.

That particular chore involved carrying a large cardboard box — the purported sea bat's cage — back to the designated area and setting it down gingerly. Since most of the crewmen on board *Coucal* already knew the joke, everyone gathered around to watch.

The Marine, however, did not have a clue.

Following a long and involved build-up to the sea bat's revealing, included the Chief throwing a lettuce leaf or two into the bat's cage, it was stressed to the Marine that if he looked directly into the box, he would scare the sea bat.

As if on cue, the Marine demanded he be allowed to look into the cage.

"Well, if you insist," the Chief responded.

"But be very careful that you don't scare it. We don't want a scared sea bat fluttering around the ship!"

As the Marine bent over to look into the box, the Chief whacked the Marine firmly on his exposed backside with a straw broom.

The blow's force nearly lifted that Marine off the deck.

I would venture to say, that is one Marine who never forgot the time he saw a sea bat while serving aboard the *USS Coucal*.

Meanwhile, everyone else enjoyed a hearty laugh at the Marine's expense.

Chapter 118

Complete Turnaround

By the time we returned the *Coucal* to port in Pearl Harbor, I could sense a massive and collective change in the attitude of almost everyone in the crew towards the ship and its officers.

There was a palpable upward turn in onboard morale.

As it was getting close to Christmas, Executive Officer Ben Benites asked me if I would allow the crew to decorate the ship for the holiday.

Neither he nor I saw any problem with the idea of decorations as long as they did not restrict us in any way from getting underway and performing our mission if we were suddenly called out of port for any reason.

I continued about my own business for the remainder of the duty day, and then debarked for the evening looking forward to some private time with my wife Mary Lou and our two boys.

By the next morning, I had nearly forgotten about the decoration request until I returned to the pier and focused my eyes on the *Coucal*. I could not believe what I saw.

The ship's exhaust stack was painted to resemble a gigantic barber pole and someone had placed a cutout of Santa Claus sitting on top of that same stack and appearing ready to slide down the chimney.

Right away, I began to worry about the reaction our ship decorations might bring from the powers that be up on the hill.

Well, all my worry was for nothing as not one word was ever said by the base commander or his staff.

In fact, the *Coucal* won a prize as the best decorated ship of its class in the entire Pearl Harbor area.

The prize was much appreciated by the ship's crew as it included a year's subscription to *Playboy* magazine.

Needless to say, the positive recognition that went along with the prize was a suitable reward for the crew's efforts.

Chapter 119

Plebe Orientation

During the ensuing holiday period as I relaxed with family and friends, my memories again wandered back to my days aboard the *USS Pomfret*.

The *Pomfret*'s wardroom consisted of five Naval Academy graduates including Captain Nuss. Also included was another fine officer with a master's degree in engineering from Rensselaer Polytechnic Institute. Finally, there was Herb Burton, who received a fine education from Auburn University.

Among those seven officers with their college educations, I could compete only by expending vast amounts of time, energy and effort.

To make up for my educational shortcomings, the Naval Academy graduates offered to provide me an abbreviated plebe or freshman year orientation, much like the ones they had each endured.

For example, I had to know what is written on a Naval Academy belt buckle. — Hint: fidelity is up and obedience is down — and the slang name for meat loaf. Back then, meat loaf was called African trail markers. Alas, I'm sure that name is no longer politically correct nor acceptable.

This hazing period was a lot of fun and brought us all closer together as a unit.

Chapter 120

Friendship versus Professionalism

My friendship with then-Lieutenant Commander Herb Burton best demonstrates those sensitive areas that sometimes come between friendship and professionalism.

Herb and his wonderful wife Pat, who has since passed on, and I and my wife Mary Lou were very close friends whenever we were off the submarine. Our homes in San Diego were within three or four miles of each other.

At that time, I owned an old Ford pickup truck that Herb and I used to commute to and from work at the Navy base.

But when we were on the boat, Herb was the Executive Officer and therefore my boss.

As part of my training, Herb corrected me very often. I readily admit that I needed his correction, but I still resented it.

On board the submarine, I could see no reason to speak to Herb except in the line of duty. That attitude carried over to our commuting in the truck both directions.

Once we were home, however, our families would get together several times each week during our off-duty times. That was when Herb and I would once again become the best of friends.

Monday mornings, however, when we were back in the truck together and heading to the boat, I really could see no reason to converse with Herb.

We would ride in stony silence, our minds focused on our various individual duties aboard the *Pomfret*.

Many times throughout the remainder of my career, I have called upon Herb Burton and other former commanding officers for training and guidance to keep me on the right track.

My successes, however slight, were because of Herb Burton and several other officers like him.

I love him as a brother to this day.

Chapter 121

What is Your Call Sign?

"Diving Officer, I believe we are airborne!"
Officer of the Deck, Underway
Status report during a surface broach
Submitted by Gene Brockingham,
ETCS (SS), US Navy (retired)

All but one of the officers on the *USS Pomfret* were most helpful and very, very patient with me.

However, there was this one officer who did not care for ex-enlisted men who were then promoted to commissioned officers.

This man was our third officer under the Captain, which made him our second Executive Officer as well as the senior Watch Officer.

When I first became qualified as an Officer of the Deck underway, I was also authorized to stand conning tower watches as the Officer of the Deck submerged. My duties then involved observing the ocean's surface through the periscope.

One time while we were at sea and submerged off the coast of San Diego, we were working closely with the Submarine Flotilla One's sound boat as they were conducting sonar tests to see whether our submarine had any particular or peculiar noises that could give our position away or identify us as the *USS Pomfret*.

In operational parlance, these telltale sounds are called a signature.

Any boat with a tell-tale signature was a big hazard when conducting operations at sea. For more on this topic, I again refer you to the book *Blind Man's Bluff*.

As part of this operation, the *Pomfret* had to maintain almost constant communications via our underwater telephone with the sound boat.

Anyway, I was calling the sound boat periodically and was using the widely accepted phraseology, "Sound Boat, Sound Boat. This is Interfere."

Interfere was the *Pomfret*'s identifying call sign.

The operator on board the sound boat would then reply and we would get on with the next required test.

Well, the above mentioned officer who thought I should have remained an enlisted man came up into the conning tower and immediately jumped on me for not using the proper Navy call sign for the sound boat.

When it was my turn once again to use the underwater telephone, I asked, "Sound Boat, Sound Boat. What is your call sign?"

"Interfere, Interfere. My call sign is Sound Boat!" the operator responded.

Well, the officer was embarrassed and I was once again in the craps with him.

Chapter 122

Ship in Distress?

During this same training period on *Pomfret*, I was once again pulling service duty as the Officer of the Deck underway. We were steaming along on the surface with nothing much happening.

During such lulls in activity, often a light and humorous mood would help break the monotony of being on board and away from home.

Well, I heard a voice coming up from below in the conning tower.

"Permission to come to the bridge," the voice said.

"Permission granted," I replied since we were not expecting to dive.

So up comes an electricians' mate by the name of Summers.

"Lieutenant Gibson, what does it mean when a ship flies the ensign (American flag) upside down?"

"Well, Summers," I replied, "on a merchant ship, it can mean the ship is in distress."

"And if you can't find an Ensign," Summers continued, "will a Lieutenant Junior Grade do?"

I summarily excused his crude pun and ordered him to return below.

Chapter 123

Shopping Cart Races

Executive Officer Herb Burton had extreme trust in me and was super supportive. He was totally in my corner, although at times I was not so sure.

As I mentioned, I did not like him correcting me, especially when he really held my feet to the fire as any good officer should and must do. This was especially true when I was in training as a freshly caught brand-new officer.

During this time frame, I went from torpedo and gunnery officer to being engineering officer.

My previous stint as an ex-engineman was of great value now that I was charge of the engineering department.

By this time in its many years of service, the *USS Pomfret* was in dire need of a thorough shipyard overhaul. So we entered Mare Island Naval Shipyard for the next six months.

Mary Lou and our sons moved back up to Vallejo to be with me during this period. Instead of living with her folks, however, we opted instead to live in a federally owned World War II apartment complex located just outside Mare Island.

Although somewhat old, these buildings had been converted into very livable quarters for officers and their families who were assigned to live there on a temporary status.

During this period, the boys were older and the entire family had a lot of fun, especially when I wasn't on the submarine checking on things.

One evening immediately following a party in the housing area, someone came up with the brilliant idea of shopping cart races.

These races were unique in that the men would place their wives into the basket of a four-wheeled shopping cart and couples would race each other up and down the street.

Of course, each race was accompanied by tumultuous noise and laughter.

Well, someone in the housing area apparently could not abide to see other people having so much fun.

That person called base security and their arrival put an end to any more shopping cart races during our stay at Mare Island.

Come to think of it, I do not recall there ever being any actual winners.

But I do remember that Johnny Walker scotch reigned supreme.

Chapter 124

Finch Strikes Again

A short time later, a new skipper by the name of Lieutenant Commander Bill Lynch reported on board the *Pomfret* and Executive Officer Herb Burton was relieved by Lieutenant Commander Wes Hogan as the boat's new Executive Officer.

By this time, I had worked my way up through the various departments to become the Engineering Officer as our boat was completing its overhaul, so the family moved back down to our home in San Diego.

After a couple of test dives and a few days of retraining, the *Pomfret* soon departed Mare Island and headed once again for fleet duty in San Diego.

Upon our arrival in southern California, we tied up at a pier adjacent to the US Navy Fleet Sonar School.

From there, Captain Lynch and I went up on the base to pay our respects to the Rear Admiral residing there.

As we neared the Admiral's residence, we noticed his personal automobile backing out of the garage.

"Isn't that one of our sailors driving the Admiral's car?" the Captain remarked as he turned to look at me in astonishment.

"That is Seaman Finch off our boat, sir," I stammered in a low voice.

Upon entering the house, the Captain addressed the Admiral.

"Sir, I think that one of my sailors just drove off in your car," he said with a great deal of embarrassment.

"Oh, that is Finch. Yes, he borrows my car quite often," the Admiral said with a laugh.

Chapter 125

Snake Ranch Christmas

Later, back in San Diego after the *Pomfret*'s repairs were completed, some of the unmarried submarine officers rented a house quickly dubbed the Snake Ranch. This residence was located across San Diego Bay on Coronado Island.

Snake Ranch residents were famous for hosting wild parties.

As the Christmas season neared, the officer's wardroom was invited to join the Snake Ranch revelries one Friday evening. One of *Pomfret*'s officers who lived at Snake Ranch decided that an authentic Christmas party needed a Santa Claus to come down the chimney.

Much later that same evening, enquiries began to circulate about the whereabouts of that same officer as he was nowhere to be found.

Well, as the evening wound down, there was finally a lull in the noise and someone heard a faint cry of "Help! Help!" emanating from the stone chimney. Apparently, the missing officer had decided to play Santa and was stuck while climbing halfway down inside the chimney.

The fire department was eventually called. They dismantled the fireplace stone by stone in order to free the culprit.

Chapter 126

Stay-at-Home Mom

Several more weeks of submarine training were in the mix for the *Pomfret* as we were now in the final throes of getting ready to go back to the Western Pacific on another six month deployment.

For this or any WestPac trip, preparations are always far-reaching.

We would be thousands of miles from our homes and away from all of our normal sources of supply. We also would be away from our families for an extended period, so the wives were also preparing to be both father and mother to their children.

It was in these situations when Mary Lou showed her true strength and grit. She was masterful in her approach to raising our two boys. We were fortunate enough that Mary Lou was able to be a stay-at-home mom. She treated those times of loneliness as her job to care for our home, finances and family.

She was also very involved with the wives of both enlisted and commissioned officers from the *Pomfret*, our buddy boat and any other submarines that might be located in San Diego. The wives and dependent families could turn to the local submarine crew members from these other boats if any needs arose.

Otherwise, the ladies would plan get-togethers and attend various submarine base-sponsored events held at the Ballast Point Submarine Officers Club out on Point Loma.

Chapter 127

Speedy Diet Plan

With the *Pomfret* fully loaded, we said our goodbyes and once again cleared the San Diego Harbor.

We set sail for Pearl Harbor and eventually Yokosuka, Japan, for a six-month WestPac tour.

Living in close quarters with six to ten officers and a crew of 70-71 enlisted men, a submariner quickly learns that one should never utter a statement, whether onboard or ashore with shipmates, that you don't want to hear or live with the consequences later.

Ignoring such sage advice, one of our sailors whom I shall call "Speedy" boldly declared he would lose 20 pounds during our trip to Japan.

Well, Speedy bunked in the aft torpedo room, so after Speedy started his diet, every so often one of the sailors removed Speedy's webbed belt as he slept.

With a very sharp razor, the sailor shaved a little bit off the buckle end of Speedy's fabric belt to reduce its size.

During the course of the voyage, Speedy began to notice that despite his every effort to lose weight, his belt only seemed to get tighter and tighter.

That and his personal resolve caused Speedy to eat less and less.

Well, I am happy to report that with the crewman's stealthy assistance, Speedy did reach his goal — and even managed to lose a little bit extra.

Chapter 128

Overcome by Smoke

We had an uneventful transit of the Pacific and arrived safely in Yokosuka where we commenced an arrival upkeep and repair period.

Once again, the *Pomfret* was moored at Pier One for routine maintenance. That was where our main engine was being tuned up. Well, when it was started up following the repairs, our main engine went out of control and filled the entire boat with diesel smoke until the engine was shut down.

A fine sailor, P. R. Reva, courageously entered the forward engine room to shut down the engine. However, Captain Lynch and I were overcome by the thick black smoke that came rolling into the control room.

We were evacuated from the ship and each of us eventually recovered with no lasting effects.

In the end, it all came out to the good and a lot was learned by all of us from that one incident.

During our six month stay in WestPac, we made several port visits including brief stops in Hong Kong and Subic Bay in the Philippine Islands.

The *Pomfret* then returned to Yokosuka and we used our remaining time in port to prepare for our return voyage to San Diego.

Chapter 129

Rubbing Shoulders With Stars

While we were out of the picture, Mary Lou and some of the *Pomfret* wives had several adventures back in San Diego.

As it so happened, the submarine area base commander happened to be friends with several Hollywood movie stars. He had invited Cary Grant, Tony Curtis and Rock Hudson to come on a tour of the base on April 11, 1963.

The celebrities were supposed to go out on a submarine for a short ride. Upon their return, there was to be a cocktail party arranged at the Ballast Point Submarine Officers Club, sort of an informal meet and greet for all the submarine base wives.

"The buddy boat gals called me and let me know there was going to be a cocktail party for the three visiting celebrities. My friend Pat Burton — Herb's wife — asked me whether I wanted to go with her," Mary Lou recalls.

Of course, Mary Lou agreed, but the day before the Hollywood stars were to arrive, the Navy's newest nuclear submarine, *USS Thresher* (SSN-593), went down during sea trials and sank with 129 submariners and assorted shipyard personnel on board. This was one of the worst peace-time Navy disasters for many years, and the first involving a nuclear-powered submarine.

Rock Hudson with Mary Lou Gibson, in glasses.

As a result, two movie stars — Cary Grant and Tony Curtis — backed out of the base tour and submarine ride. Rock Hudson, however, did visit the base and take the excursion.

That evening, during the cocktail party, Mary Lou and several of her friends had their photograph taken with Rock Hudson.

"He was one good-looking son of a gun, let me tell you," recalled Mary Lou, who stood at Rock Hudson's left during the photo.

"But he was kind of a wet fish in person," she noted.

Apparently, when the ladies arrived at the party, there was a receiving line of sorts so everyone could greet the celebrity in turn.

We would say, "Well, hello Mr. Hudson. How are you?"

"Fine," he responded.

"Did you enjoy your trip today?" one of the ladies asked.

"Yes," Hudson replied.

Rock Hudson

"Would you like to go out again some time?" another queried.

"Yes," Hudson said.

"It was almost as if Rock Hudson didn't know what to say unless he had a script in front of him," Mary Lou remembered.

But he was one of Mary Lou's favorite stars and she recalls seeing several of his movies including *Send Me No Flowers*, which was released the following year in 1964.

Hudson eventually appeared in 70 films and launched a successful television career in the 1970s and 1980s with a starring role in *McMillan & Wife* (1971-77) and *Dynasty*, from 1981 until his death at age 59 in 1985.

Mary Lou had other brushes with Hollywood fame thanks to her long friendship with Pat Burton, who had once been married, as Pat Dempsey, to child actor John Richard "Dickie" Moore, Jr., one of the principles in the *Our Gang* movie short series that later was turned into the *Little Rascals* television show. Pat was the mother of Dick Moore's only son, Kevin.

John Richard "Dickie"

Pat Dempsey's friends in high school included Elizabeth Taylor and Jane Powell. Powell ended up marrying Dick Moore in 1988 and remained his wife until Dick Moore's death in 2015 at age 89.

Pat Burton would also keep Mary Lou up to date on when different celebrities would come to town.

When Roddy McDowall came to visit, Pat introduced Mary Lou to Roddy, who happened to be godfather to Pat Burton's son, Kevin.

Chapter 130

Flying Submariner

Meanwhile, back on *Pomfret*, the crew and I spent several weeks at sea and enjoyed a stop in Pearl Harbor before arriving back in San Diego.

We resumed normal operations while conducting training exercises in the Pacific Ocean waters around San Diego. During one of these operations, the *Pomfret* was working with a battle group that included the anti-submarine warfare aircraft carrier *USS Kearsarge* (CV-33).

Since my command specialty was Submarine Evasion Tactics. Captain Lynch decided that I could learn a lot about anti-submarine warfare if I spent a few days on the carrier.

USS Kearsarge (CV-33) underway   US Navy photo

He received permission for my temporary transfer to the carrier. There was just one hitch.

How was I, a submariner, to get to the aircraft carrier?
On the day of transfer, the carrier Commander sent a helicopter to fetch me to my temporary new home.

Helicopter prepares for personnel transfer.   US Navy photo

Did I mention that I am very afraid of heights?

This helicopter trip was not something I really wanted to do. But there was the helicopter crew, hovering over our surfaced submarine and lowering a line to our deck.

I struggled into the harness and was hoisted up with a winch to the open door of the helicopter and flown to the carrier's landing deck. Once safely on the carrier's wide flight deck, I was escorted to the flag officer's area where I met the officer attached to the anti-submarine warfare staff.

My host officer and his staff were most hospitable and did their best to give me their full attention in showing me around their area and in explaining all of the functions they performed while searching for submarines.

I spent three days aboard the aircraft carrier. I went roaming throughout that huge ship and got lost several times. But eventually I had to return to my submarine, the *Pomfret*.

The transfer back would be by the same helicopter, but by his time the seas had picked up and the ocean was pretty choppy.

The helicopter was bouncing around in the wind quite a bit which didn't help my nerves. Once we were hovering over the submarine, the helicopter crew fastened me into the lowering harness.

Oh my!

I looked out the open door of the aircraft and way down below, there was the forward deck of my submarine. It was only about 18 feet across, but from that height, it looked extremely small to me on that particular day.

Crew members prepare to assist in personnel transfer.   US Navy photo

While I was positioning myself to get lowered, somehow my suitcase fell out the open door of the helicopter and splashed into the ocean, never to be seen again.

At this point, the helicopter crew had to help me — a polite way of saying they pushed me — out of the helicopter and lowered the line until I was dangling in midair. Meanwhile, the ocean was causing the submarine's forward deck to bounce and sway below me.

The wind was blowing spray from the wave tops into my eyes as the helicopter crew maneuvered me into the waiting arms of my submarine crew members, who were waiting on deck to wrestle me out of my harness.

My feet finally touched the submarine's deck and I ran as fast as I could for the aft deck access port. I wanted to get below and out of the wind-blown salt spray as rapidly as possible.

As far as I'm concerned, the Navy would have to forget helicopters for this sailor from then on.

Chapter 131

Cooper River Desk Job

Eventually, my nearly four years on board the *USS Pomfret* came to an end and it was time for Navy Lieutenant Jim Gibson to move along to yet another assignment. My new orders were to be part of the office staff for a newly formed unit, Commander Submarine Squadron Eighteen, headquartered in Charleston, South Carolina.

This was to be the first Polaris missile submarine squadron to be located in the United States. Until that time, these missile carrying submarines were previously based out of Holy Loch, Scotland.

A ballistic missile submarine can launch ballistic missiles (SLBMS) equipped with nuclear warheads, even while submerged. The US Navy's hull classification symbols for such boats are SSB and SSBN. The SS denotes submarine or submersible ship. The B stands for ballistic missile and the N denotes nuclear power.

I first reported to Commander Submarine Flotilla Six, also stationed in Charleston for temporary duty. For the next two months I was assigned duties as a flotilla watch officer.

Soon after, Submarine Squadron Eighteen was commissioned or called into service in August of 1964, we moved up the Cooper River — locals pronounce it Cuppa River — to the Cooper River Fleet Ballistic Missile Replenishment Site in Charleston.

The Navy had built a pier protruding into the river. A brand new submarine tender, the *USS Simon Lake* (AS-33), was moored there after successfully navigating the Cooper River, no easy task in itself.

We now moved on board the tender as the brand new Submarine Squadron Eighteen.

It was the staff's responsibility to care for and administer aid to the submarines attached to our squadron. I was to be the Assistant Material Officer for Squadron Eighteen.

The Material Officer has responsibility for anything to do with the mechanical requirements when submarines are alongside and attached to our squadron.

The *USS Simon Lake* had the capability of caring for Polaris missiles and the submarines that carried them. This submarine tender was brand new and totally up to date and as modern as was possible at that time.

She even had one of the first shipboard computers in the entire Atlantic Fleet.

I say a computer, but really it was a series of IBM punch card readers connected to a room full of sensitive electronics. This system, while very primitive, was also revolutionary for 1964.

The computing machinery for this system took up an entire deck of this large ship. By inserting times and data of repair items on these punch cards, we could for the very first time predict the man hours needed to complete a particular repair.

As an added benefit, any parts needed to complete the repair could be ordered or even manufactured, if that was necessary, in order to complete the work as scheduled.

This was done because these Polaris-carrying submarines were the mainstay of our nation's deterrent force during the Cold War. As such, they always had to be ready to set sail on time.

Chapter 132

Blue and Gold Coordinator

After living for a time in Charleston proper, our family moved into MenRiv Park Housing near Monk's Corner, South Carolina, just outside the Naval Weapons Station Charleston, now designated as Naval Support Activity Charleston. This weapons facility is located on the west bank of the Cooper River in the cities of Goose Creek and Hanahan, SC.

This posting was a great one for me and the family. We lived in federal housing on the Naval Weapons Station.

The boys were enrolled in local schools and involved in lots of activities including Cub Scouts and Boy Scouts. Mary Lou worked with the boys on lots of projects including as a Cub Scout Den Mother for the local Cub Scout Pack. Later, she became the person responsible for coordinating changes in Scout leaders between each of the nuclear submarines' Blue and Gold crews.

Since Polaris-equipped submarines are constantly on the prowl, they are assigned two complete crews. The Blue crew heads out for the first 90 days, then the Gold crew swaps duty for the next 90-day stint. Hence the nickname of "90-day wonders" for members of these crews.

When the Pack Cubmaster or Boy Scout Troop Leader from the Blue crew went to sea, she had to call on the Gold crew leader to come to meetings and take over.

Just like the buddy boat system on the diesel submarines in San Diego, Mary Lou could rely on assistance from members of either the Blue or Gold crews while I was at sea.

This arrangement was quite nice, especially when a washing machine went out. Mary Lou would just call one of the guys in port who would come over to repair it and get it running again.

Close to our house, we had many of nature's creatures including alligators, raccoons and every form of biting bug or poisonous snake known to man in that region. All of this wildlife helped make the local fishing great beyond belief.

The boys and I had a beautiful wooden boat with an outboard motor installed and we did our share of fishing.

We even took Mother out with us once. But when she out-fished us, she was never invited again.

Just kidding!

Chapter 133

Field of Dreams

During my stay in Charleston, I worked under the very capable command of Lieutenant Commander Chris Brown, who coincidentally was on the examining board for my selection to Ensign when I was attending and teaching at the Nuclear Power Training Unit in Arco, Idaho.

He probably said several times that all of his chickens were coming home to roost.

During this time, sailors attached to the tender as well as those in the submarine crews traveled into Charleston for liberty. This was a trip of more than 20 miles on an extremely dangerous highway.

Our Commodore, Captain Randy Moore, was very sensitive to the welfare of his enlisted men and officers. He believed strongly that if there were adequate athletic fields and recreation areas for the men to use there on the site and close to the pier, that many of the accidents and some of the road dangers could be reduced.

He called me up to his cabin and asked me whether I had any ideas to alleviate this situation. After looking into the possibilities and working out some details with the Weapons Station's public works officer, we came up with what was later to be called Gibson Field.

Using several crew members from the *USS Simon Lake*, we called on reserve Seabee units throughout the East coast and mid-Atlantic region to recruit those men who wanted to use their two-weeks of active duty to work on our project. We borrowed equipment and manpower from all over that region. I even recruited my two civilian sons to do some of the work.

Even my sons, Bill and Rich, at right, helped out.

Together, we constructed a football field and other sports facilities in what was, just three months prior, 28 acres of snake-infested swampy marshland.

One morning during construction, the Captain of the Charleston Naval Station called me and asked whether he could borrow his bulldozer back for a few days.

Another time, when Commodore Moore was showing a visiting senior officer around the site, the officer asked, "Why do I see an officer running a bulldozer out there on the field beside the pier?"

"That's Lieutenant Gibson, my assistant Material Officer," the Commodore replied.

When the project was finally complete, we had two softball fields and four tennis courts as well as a lighted football field. We cut the trees down to make poles to hold the field lights.

The facilities were always well used and one of the softball fields was named Gibson Field in my honor.

This is a very short description of a project that involved a lot of dedicated people working many hours, even during their off-duty time, over a period of four months.

Chapter 134

Gibson Field Commendation

Upon completion of the project, I was awarded a Commander Submarine Force US Atlantic Fleet Commendation:

24 May 1966
The Commander Submarine Force US Atlantic Fleet
Takes pleasure in commending
Lieutenant James W. Gibson
United States Navy

For services as set forth in the following:

CITATION

For exceptionally meritorious achievement during the period of January through March 1966 while serving on the Staff of Commander Submarine Squadron Eighteen.
As a Collateral duty, you coordinated and supervised the construction of the Recreational Facility at the Cooper River FBM replenishment Site.
Through judicious use of available manpower, materials and non-appropriated funds, you achieved a very significant savings to the government and were instrumental in providing a facility which will have a most beneficial impact

on the moral and physical well-being of personnel at the Cooper River Site for many years to come. Your enthusiasm, leadership, and Managerial competence in accomplishing this task were in keeping with the traditions of the Submarine Force and the United States Naval Service.

Signed: *V.L. LOWRANCE*
Vice Admiral, U.S. Navy

Chapter 135

Extended Road Trip

During this heavy construction period out on the site, I still had to complete my primary responsibilities of Assistant Material Officer and squadron duty officer every seven days.

While on this tour of duty, I rode several Polaris-carrying nuclear submarines as a staff officer for short periods to observe and evaluate the submarine's performance at sea.

Coming from my former duty on 20-year-old to 30-year-old diesel-powered submarines, these nuclear monsters were a thing of beauty.

But they were also in a very different world than what I was used to.

As my time in Charleston drew to a close at Squadron Eighteen in late-August 1966, I was ordered to the *USS Catfish* (SS-339) home ported in San Diego, California.

I took some leave time so that the family and I could motor across the northern part of the United States and southern Canada.

This extended road trip was scenic and, to a point, restful.

It was a wonderful time for me to be with Mary Lou and our two rapidly growing boys, Billy and Richard. While touring, we stopped every evening so the boys could swim in a motel pool.

The high point of our road trip was visiting Mount Rushmore in South Dakota. We could not believe the size and beauty of this massive national monument.

The nearby Crazy Horse Memorial was just starting construction about that time, so we stopped by to see it as well.

The Crazy Horse Memorial is a mountain monument under construction on privately held land in the Black Hills, in Custer County, South Dakota. When completed, it will depict the Oglala Lakota warrior, Crazy Horse, riding a horse and pointing into the distance.

Crazy Horse Memorial, maquette

The memorial is operated by the Crazy Horse Memorial Foundation, a nonprofit organization.

Chapter 136

Unexpected Problems

As recounted in earlier chapters, I had joined the *USS Catfish* during a major upheaval in command to turn around a morale problem. That was certainly a team effort, of which I played a small part.

During my time on *Catfish*, however, I gained quite a reputation for solving difficult mechanical and engineering problems as well. Along the way, age and youthful indiscretions regarding my physical well-being also began to creep into the equation.

Prior to departing San Diego, the boat's sonar man made one final check with the flotilla's Sound Boat to see whether the *Catfish* had any peculiar noises while underway, either on the surface or submerged. That test revealed our port-side propeller was making a heavy noise that could be heard at some distance.

The noisy propeller had to be replaced during the *USS Catfish*'s forthcoming stop in Pearl Harbor while en route to Japan.

Departure day finally arrived and the pier was awash with our crew members saying goodbye to their families and the squadron personnel staying behind with our buddy boat.

We cast off the mooring lines and departed San Diego, pointing the *Catfish* due west on the first leg of our trip en route to Hawaii. It was a very smooth trip with lots of underway training, although I did notice a growing pain in my right knee.

Submarine in a floating dry dock

After arriving at the Submarine Base in Pearl Harbor, the boat entered the floating dry-dock for replacement of our port side propeller.

This left us with one major problem: refueling the submarine. The Catfish needed to have all her fuel tanks full and topped off prior to departing Pearl Harbor. Under normal circumstances with the submarine afloat, most of the empty tanks would be full of sea water.

During the refueling process, fuel would be pumped into the tanks and any sea water ballast remaining in those tanks would be forced out and over the side. However, we couldn't take time to do this once the new propeller was installed because we were slotted for a very important mission almost as soon as we arrived in Yokosuka, Japan.

This unexpected propeller replacement was making our transit schedule very tight as it was without adding more time for refueling.

Chapter 137

Dry Dock Refueling Test

Along with the boat's entire Engineering Department, I decided that we would need to refuel while in dry dock due to our scheduling problems. Our new propeller would need to be sound tested as soon as we departed the submarine base and that meant there was no other time available to refuel except while in dry dock.

I discussed all of this with the boat's fuel oil king, the sailor in charge of our on-board oil systems, as well as with the officer in charge of the dry dock.

Together, we came up with a way to fuel the boat while she was still in dry dock.

We hooked up a long hose to our fuel filling and compensating system. As the new fuel was pushed into the tanks, the water in those tanks was pumped into a waste-water barge that we had moved adjacent to the floating dry dock.

We received permission from the Officer in Charge of the floating dry dock to fuel the boat using this method.

To do so safely, however, we had to place several men at strategic points on the *Catfish* to watch out for any fire or flooding problems.

We were able to complete the entire hours-long refueling process at about the same time as the propeller replacement job was being completed.

While this was all taking place, our skipper, Captain Varley, was invited to sit in on the morning staff briefing hosted by the Commander Pacific Submarine Force. Captain Varley had recently been a member of this staff prior to reporting on board the Catfish. Following the briefing, Captain Varley stayed behind to speak privately with the Admiral.

In the course of their conversation, the Admiral asked how the propeller change was going.

"It's going just fine, and I can report that we are almost ready to get underway," Varley replied.

The admiral then asked about the need for refueling.

"Refueling is complete, Admiral," the Captain reported with a grin. The Admiral was in shock. He had never heard of a submarine being fueled while in dry dock.

"Well, sir, you have never met my Engineering Officer, Jim Gibson!" Captain Varley said.

Chapter 138

Deep Knee Pain

The *Catfish* finally departed the repair area and we all said Aloha once again to Pearl Harbor as we started our transit to WestPac. As our boat cleared the harbor, we met up as planned with a sound boat.

The *Catfish* submerged and ran a short way so the sound boat could complete its test of our new propeller while underway as well as while submerged. Everything checked out satisfactorily, so we surfaced and thanked the sound boat before pointing our bow once again to the far west.

During our at-sea transit to Japan, my right knee started to become very sore. It also ballooned up in severe swelling so that I had trouble walking.

This was apparently due to all those days in my youth when I pushed my small, light frame to play football matched against opponents much larger and heavier than myself.

When the *Catfish* was at sea, both of my knees would start to act up. But the right knee was in much worse shape than was the left.

When we arrived in Yokosuka, I was sent to a nearby Naval Hospital so my knees could be evaluated. The only answer the medical staff would give me was to come off of sea duty.

Well, this was not a happy time for me, nor did it sit well with the boat's company.

The *Catfish* was scheduled to take part in an important special operation.

This was not a good time for the boat to lose its Engineering Officer and Battle Stations Diving Officer of the Deck.

Chapter 139

Take the *Hake* for Knee Relief

Despite my protests, I was ordered off the *USS Catfish* and transferred as Officer in Charge of the *USS Hake* (SS-256), a World War II-era submarine, now retired and no longer a sea-going vessel.

The *Hake* was berthed at the Naval Shipyard in Philadelphia, Pennsylvania. There it served as a training station for the US Navy Reserve ,Unit 4-37. The senior command there was the Commandant of the Fourth Naval District.

Upon leaving the crew of the *Catfish* behind, I flew from Japan to Los Angeles. While en route, we touched down briefly on Wake Island, made famous during World War II.

Wake is located two-thirds of the way between Honolulu and Guam. From the air, the shape of the island resembles the wake of a ship plowing through the ocean.

The reason for this stop escapes me now, but I was impressed that Wake is one very small island.

When you approach the island it looks like there is nothing but water until the plane's wheels touch down on the runway's surface.

Administered by the United States Air Force under an agreement with the U. S. Department of the Interior, the center of activity on the atoll is at Wake Island Airfield, primarily used as a mid-Pacific refueling stop for military aircraft and as an emergency landing area. The 9,800-foot runway is the longest strategic runway in the Pacific Islands.

During this time and while I was still en-route to the United States, my mother suffered a massive stroke in Pennsylvania.

After spending a short homecoming with my wife, Mary Lou, and our two sons in San Diego, I motored to my parent's home in Mount Jackson, Penn.

While there, I spent time with my father and visited my mother in the hospital. As it turned out, those were some of the last days my mother would spend with both of us.

Mom passed away about six weeks later.

Chapter 140

Winning the Nimitz Trophy

After finally reporting to the Naval Reserve section of Commandant Fourth Naval District, I took on my assigned duties as Officer in Charge of the submarine *Hake* while doubling up as Senior Instructor for the Navy Reserve, Unit 4-37.

While there, I had a staff of ten highly qualified enlisted submariners who served as the station's keepers. Under my charge, these men supported and trained the Navy Reserve's submarine unit personnel.

The Navy Reserve submarine unit was made up of qualified former submariners, both officers and enlisted men, who completed the required drilling time needed to keep their submarine knowledge current while training on board the *Hake*.

The reservists would spend one weekend a month on the submarine to practice various evolutions as prescribed in the Navy Reserve's submarine training manual. They did so under the watchful eyes and careful supervision of the regular Navy personnel and myself.

Once a year, these same Navy reservists would be ordered to active duty for training. During that time, they would then spend two weeks at sea on a fleet submarine.

With 42 Navy Reserve submarine units scattered throughout the United States, there were plenty of reservists to train. Each reserve

USS Hake was used to train Naval Reservists in Unit 4-37.

unit was also given a yearly inspection and graded relative to the other units.

In 1969 and while under my command, Naval Reserve Unit 4-37 was awarded the Fleet Admiral Nimitz trophy as the best Navy Reserve submarine unit in the United States.

This was due in large part to the many dedicated reservists who passed through our training program as well as my hard working regular Navy station keepers. The trophy represented a big feather in each of our hats.

Our Navy Reserve unit's Commanding Officer, Captain Joseph Loughran, was one of the most dedicated, hard-working officers with whom I ever served. Believe it or not, he was a sure enough Philadelphia lawyer in his civilian capacity.

Captain Loughran spent many days without pay during his reserve time working with me at the boat to improve his unit.

All of our hard work eventually paid off handsomely when the Nimitz Trophy was finally presented.

Chapter 141

Small Ship
Training Officer

During this time and because of staff officer transfers throughout the Command Fourth Naval District, I was given additional duty as Small Ship Training Officer for our entire district.

This was on top of my duties with the Navy Reserve's Submarine Training Unit and managing the programs taking place on *USS Hake*. My extra work and added responsibilities also included quite a bit of travel.

The small training ships were Patrol Craft stationed at various ports on the Great Lakes and included one other decommissioned submarine, the *USS Cod* (SS-224), moored at a commercial pier on Lake Erie in Cleveland, Ohio.

This was a demanding job requiring me to travel all over the East Coast and up on the Great Lakes. During this time, the *Hake* was taken for disposal and replaced by the *USS Angler* (SS-240).

During World War II, the *Angler* was ordered to the southern Philippine Island of Panay to rescue 20 persons held by Japanese forces. When the submarine arrived off Panay, however, its captain and crew quickly learned that instead of saving 20 people, there were actually 58 men, women and children in need rescue.

The refugees were crowded on board somehow and the *Angler* and its crew delivered all of them to safety.

Chapter 142

City of Brotherly Love

My duty stay in Philadelphia was very good for our entire family. We lived on the base in very nicely refurbished ex-Prisoner of War barracks.

The base had excellent amenities. It was equipped with a Commissary, a Navy Exchange, a movie theater and many other diversions to keep us entertained and occupied.

Our sons Bill and Rich attended classes in the Philadelphia public school system. The boys also enjoyed all types of extracurricular activities on the Navy base.

In the summer, they swam in the base pool. During the winter they ice skated on a parking lot hosed down with fresh water and allowed to freeze over.

Both boys were involved in Boy Scouts. Their scout troop's various projects added to the many interests enjoyed by our sons.

Mary Lou soon learned that life in Philadelphia also had its down side.

"There were a few duty stations that I didn't like. One of them was Philadelphia, Pennsylvania," she recalls.

It turns out that organized crime families, many connected to the Mafia, had taken up residence in Philadelphia as well.

One particular day that stands out in Mary Lou's memory was when her son Bill came home from school with an announcement.

"Mom, Freddie offered me a cigarette!"

Other boys hanging around Freddie had suggested to Bill that the cigarette Freddie was selling actually contained marijuana.

"I told him I didn't smoke. Then they said Freddie would give it to me. So then I told them I still didn't want it," Bill told his anxious mother.

"Thank God he didn't accept it," Mary Lou said of her son.

Always frugal with his money, Bill told his mother that at the price Freddie was asking for that one cigarette, it would cost him $42 for an entire carton of smokes.

To keep the boys occupied in more acceptable activities, Mary Lou arranged for Bill to take piano lessons after school hours while Rich learned to play a guitar. Even at the building where her son took piano lessons, Mary Lou would frequently see Mafia guys running their numbers (gambling) racket.

"I swear, my boys have seen it all," she recalled.

Similarly, son Rich came home from sixth grade one day while the family was in Philadelphia and invited his mother to attend a school program featuring one of Rich's friends.

She attended the program, and right in front of parents and the other students, Rich's friend stood up, rolled up both of his shirt sleeves and addressed the audience.

"Moms and Dads, I want you to see my arms. I started smoking marijuana in kindergarten. I would use my milk money to buy it. These scars (indicating marks visible on both of his forearms) are needle tracks from mainlining heroin. But I'm okay now!" announced the sixth-grade student.

Chapter 143

Sounding the Alarm

To counteract these negative influences, I created opportunities to take my boys for overnight stays aboard our training submarine.

On one such visit, my son Richard awoke at about 3 a.m. and somehow managed to press a lever sounding the submarine's diving alarm. This activated a loud klaxon that blared a hellish "AaaUUUggaaa" similar to the horn of a Model T Ford, but much louder. The alarm also awoke the Chief who had been sleeping soundly.

The following day, when I reported for work, the Chief strongly suggested that Rich should never again be allowed on an overnight visit.

Of course, as the boy's parent, I was very concerned. Afterwards, however, my son and I had a good laugh over the incident.

Also while our family stayed in Philadelphia, several of our weekends involved journeys to the western part of the state so we could visit my father, who was then a widower.

On a few occasions, I even managed to get up there to hunt pheasants in the Mount Jackson area with some of my Dad's friends and a few of our other relatives.

That same year, I shot and killed a large white tailed deer while I and two of my relatives were hunting with friends near the small north-central Pennsylvania town of Bradford.

That town and the surrounding area is well known for its beautiful fall foliage when the tree leaves turn many shades of red, yellow, orange and brown.

Chapter 144

Pennsylvania Crude

While hunting in Pennsylvania, we usually stayed on a farm well known for its scenic beauty.

The farmer would rent out the upstairs of his machine shop for hunting parties to use for sleeping quarters. His wife provided very fine meals for all of us. She even packed a box lunch for our noon meal spent out in the woods.

The farmer was a very tough old mountain man. He had a pet fox that was very tame. He kept it tied up to a dog house. Every time the farmer came outside, the fox would run into his shelter until the farmer could coax him out.

Apparently, when the farmer first caught the fox, the fox bit him on the hand just as the farmer went to pet it. The farmer was not pleased, so he picked up the fox and took him into the machine shed. There, he ground off the sharp points of the foxes' teeth.

"The fox never offered to bite me again!" the farmer told us.

This area of the state is where Pennsylvania pure crude oil is found. To illustrate how pure this oil was, this same farmer had an oil well on his place with a separating tank down by the barn.

The separating tank was used to settle out any water that came up out of the ground along with the crude oil. Since water and oil do not mix, the water would sink and the oil would float on top.

One morning, we watched the farmer pull his tractor over to the separating tank. He then used a dipper to take a scoop of this crude, non-refined oil, out of the tank and pour it directly into his tractor's engine. Then he resumed his field work.

The time I was able to spend up there away from my Navy duties was a wonderful and relaxing vacation.

Chapter 145

After-Hours Research

From this pleasant memory, my recollections quickly returned me to the time I attended the Navy's Deep Diving School in nearby Washington, DC. While there, I wanted to learn as much as I could from those who had served aboard submarine rescue ships such as the *USS Coucal*, where I was soon to take on my first command.

Most of my previous time in the Navy had been spent on submarines, so I was eager to learn about life on board a surface vessel.

At the diving school, there were several fine Chief Petty Officers among the students and teaching staff who had spent years at sea aboard similar ships.

Some nights after school, I would ask one or more of the Chiefs to invite me to the Chief's Club — one had to be invited — where I would spring for their beers in order to get their stories started.

Their reminiscing allowed me to ask each Chief about the various ships on which each had served. Then I would ask them about danger signs to look for in terms of poor maintenance and low morale.

Of all the problems the different chiefs mentioned, the most serious and most often mentioned was a lack of communication within a ship's crew. Most said that the officers did not keep the chiefs informed of what they desired or what was planned for the ship's future.

To gain further knowledge, I also devoured a copy of *Command at Sea* written by Rear Admiral Harley Francis Cope.

The version I read had been revised and updated by Captain Howard Bucknell, III, a fine submarine officer.

This book was almost a tutorial on how to have a successful command. I wholeheartedly recommend it for anyone interested in going to a command level.

Chapter 146

Monumental Climb

I remembered as well that during my six-month course at the deep diving school, Mary Lou and our two boys toured and re-toured the nation's capital and all of its monuments. They claim to have seen it all while I was struggling to see anything at the bottom of the silty river where we trained.

The entire six months spent in Washington, DC, proved to be a wonderful and educational time for Bill and Rich.

Photo by George Winship
Washington Monument, Washington, DC

286

For Bill, the highlight was the day he was able to climb the 898 steps and 50 landings inside the Washington Monument, all the way to its top of the 555-foot marble, granite and bluestone gneiss obelisk commemorating George Washington, a General during the American Revolution and the first President of the United States of America.

The tower has since been equipped with an elevator. Between 2005 and 2010 the monument was visited by an average of 631,000 people each year.

However, since an earthquake damaged some of the stones in 2011 and a hurricane further weakened the structure, the National Park Service has closed the monument's interior to visitors until the elevator can be modernized for longevity and safety.

It is expected to reopen in the spring of 2019.

To this day, however, if we even mention the Washington Monument to Rich, his hackles go up. He was tired of that part of the Washington scene.

Chapter 147

Sailing First Class

Upon completion of Navy Deep Diving School, I was ordered to a six-week Navy Justice School in Newport, Rhode Island.

During this period, Mary Lou and our two sons drove to Mount Jackson where they spent a nice time visiting with my Dad and some of our other relatives still residing in that immediate area.

When my Justice School training was complete, I enjoyed a short visit with my father and family before I, Mary Lou and the boys motored to Vallejo for a short visit with her parents.

Then I traveled on to Pearl Harbor, Hawaii, by airplane to prepare and assume command of the *USS Coucal*.

Mary Lou and the boys waited for sea transportation and arrived a bit later.

They cruised from San Francisco to

SS Lurline offered first-class only passage.

Honolulu on board the Matson luxury liner *SS Lurline* and had a ball.

During the voyage, Mary Lou found some other submariners and wives to pal around with. The boys roamed the *Lurline* and never missed any of the ship's wonderful meals served on board.

When my family arrived in Honolulu, I had arranged for a place we all could live comfortably in an area called Little Makalopa. It was located up a hill and across the Kam Highway from the Pearl Harbor Submarine Base.

Our rented home had a beautiful view of the Pearl Harbor Base and I could even see the *Coucal*, although it was some distance away.

Chapter 148

Career on the Line

Anyone who has been in a command position knows that there comes a very serious time when a commanding officer must put his career on the line.

As mentioned previously, the *Coucal* had been mishandled and was not well cared for on a staff level for several years prior to my taking command.

During that period, the ship would arrive in port for a scheduled two-week repair and general maintenance visit. Invariably, halfway through the process, repairs would be interrupted and the crew and vessel would be ordered back out to sea without the ship ever receiving all of its necessary repairs.

To have this happen once can be dangerous for all concerned. To have it happen time and time again for a period of years was unthinkable.

And so, over a period of time and through no fault of the ship's officers and crew, mechanical systems would fail in their daily operations. This made it nearly impossible for anyone to do a commendable job.

Following the *Coucal*'s first six-month deployment to Japan and the Western Pacific, we had been at sea for a good long period.

Executive Officer Ben Benites and I, as well as all of our wardroom officers, chiefs and enlisted crew members were looking forward to returning to the Pearl Harbor Submarine Base and two weeks of mechanical repairs and general maintenance.

Well-versed in our ship's history, during the days leading up to our arrival back in port I directed each head of department to prepare and submit proposed work lists for both the base repair department and for our own on-board routine maintenance. Then, I directed the crew to disassemble anything that needed repairs as long as it would not affect the maneuvering capabilities of our ship prior to its arrival in port.

Executive Officer Benites, who had several years experience on board various submarine rescue ships including the *Coucal*, counseled me against doing this.

"Sure as hell, Captain, we will be torn apart and the staff will get us underway. We will then be left in the same shape as we were before, or worse," were his exact words.

Even though he and I disagreed on this point, I was able to convince him that my orders should be carried out to the letter.

As much and as strongly as we disagreed in private while speaking in the privacy of my own stateroom, Ben could be counted on to support me fully and completely once we had reached a decision.

The *Coucal* arrived for this very important upkeep period on the appointed day and at the appointed time.

Sure enough, five or six days into our two weeks worth of scheduled repairs, I received a telephone call from the squadron operations officer requesting that I come to see him.

At the appointed time, I went up on the base and walked into his office.

Just as my Executive Officer had predicted, the squadron officer opened with bad news.

"Jim, I am very sorry, but we are going to have to get *Coucal* underway to act as standby for a submarine during her deep dive in the Lahaina area," he said, hardly looking up at me.

Without hesitation, I took off my Captain's hat and badge and placed them forcefully on his desk.

"No, Commander! You are not going to do that to the *Coucal* this time! At least, not with this Commanding Officer," I bravely responded.

This was scary because I knew I was placing my entire Navy career up to that point on the line for my ship and its crew. The future of my career was also in jeopardy.

After exchanging some very heated words, he and I walked together down to see the Division Commander, who's office was in the same building.

Fortunately, the Division Commander agreed with me.

Now, the three of us walked together to confer with the Squadron Commander.

At that time, the Squadron Commander was Captain Jim Wilson, now retired with the rank of Vice Admiral.

After being briefed on the situation, Captain Wilson carefully weighed each of our comments.

"Commander, have Service Squadron Five send one of the fleet tugs to stand by the submarine in case we need the *Coucal*'s standby rescue kit. But let's allow Gibson to fix his ship," Captain Wilson finally said.

This time, the *Coucal* did finish her repair period within the allotted two weeks and all of her equipment was put back together and ready to go back to sea.

It is times like this when you need to have bosses who support you when your position is fair, just and right.

"Well done, Jim! But you better know right now, you only get one of those in a career," the Division Commander later counseled me.

Chapter 149

Carrot, Stick and Falcon

By this time everyone could clearly see that our training was well advanced and the crew was performing better than it had for quite some time.

As a reward, the *Coucal* was authorized to have a dependent's cruise. But this would not be the normal three-hour dependent's cruise.

Instead, all of the married men would be allowed to invite their families along on a two-day weekend jaunt to Lahaina on the island of Maui. We arranged for the families to stay on shore in some of the nearby hotels for needed privacy.

It was a fun weekend and a fitting reward for all of the hard work the crew members had performed while in port during the repair period.

As wonderful as that weekend was, it was soon time for us to prepare for another six-month deployment to the Western Pacific.

This departure required an administrative inspection by the Division Commander. Our inspection was conducted both in port on paperwork submitted and while underway to observe all operations.

The Division Commander put us through our paces including observations of our diving techniques and operation of our McCann rescue chamber.

I was very proud when the *Coucal* received a grade of excellent overall and outstanding in diving.

While sitting at my stateroom desk, I received a call from a friend serving in another part of the Pearl Harbor area. His father-in-law was Nathan Farragut Twining, a four-star General in the US Air Force and a former Chairman of the Joint Chiefs of Staff in the Defense Department from 1957 to 1960. He was the first member of the Air Force to serve as Chairman.

My friend wanted to bring General Twining and his wife over the next day to see the *Coucal* and, if possible, have lunch aboard our ship. What a great honor this will be, I informed my officers and crew.

Happily, we went to work and dressed up the ship as we awaited the arrival of our distinguished guests.

When they approached, we posted the proper amount of side buoys — sailors forming two lines — for General Twining and his party to be piped aboard with the proper tune played on the Boatswain's pipe.

General Nathan F. Twining

We gave General Twining and his party an extensive tour of the ship including a visit to the Signalman's flag bridge, then we returned to the Officer's Wardroom for lunch.

The wardroom was in perfect order.

We went right down the line with an appetizer, then soup. To end that course, everyone was presented with a beautiful salad.

The main course included steaks with a choice of doneness.

To everyone's surprise, the *Coucal*'s very accomplished kitchen stewards had carved a perfect and beautiful falcon — the Air Force's mascot — out of a very large potato and positioned it strategically on the General's steak platter.

This meal was the hit of the day.

Of course, General Twining had to have a picture of the bird and the stewards who carved it.

Chapter 150

Inquiry and Intrigue

A week or so before we were to depart for WestPac, I received a call from the Flag Lieutenant for Admiral Walter Small, Commander of Submarines in the Pacific.

He reported that the Admiral would be down in a half-hour to take a walk through our ship.

We received him with full honors including piping him aboard with side buoys, two ranks of sailors on each side of the deck.

Admiral Small was very impressed with his visit.

The Patrol

ALERT CREW -- An Admiral passing alongside USS Coucal in his launch recently was surprised when the hard-working crew snapped into the traditional mode of rendering honors despite the fact that they were holding brooms. Presenting "brooms" are, from left, SN John Tretter, FA Kent Johnson, FA Eric Poulson, and SN Dennis Eckert.

Not long after, he was getting underway as a passenger on a submarine that was to pass alongside the *Coucal* as it backed out of its moored position.

As the submarine with the Admiral aboard passed by the *Coucal*, our entire ship's company rendered honors including four of our side cleaners standing on a small floating punt while working on the starboard side of our ship.

The Admiral thought this was so creative and unique that he had a photograph taken of those side cleaners and ordered it be published in *The Patrol*, the base newspaper.

Chapter 151

Under Investigation

During this same period, I was busy handling paperwork in my stateroom when the ship's Executive Officer, Ben Benites, knocked on the door. Ben informed me that two gentlemen in civilian clothes wanted to come in and speak with me.

After Ben ushered them into my stateroom, they introduced themselves and presented their credentials. Their first words to me came as quite a shock.

"We have checked you out, Captain, and you are clean," one of the investigators said.

If that wasn't unnerving enough, their next revelation was an even bigger surprise.

"We have, however, broken up a marijuana smuggling and sales ring on your ship!" the second man said.

Apparently, five of the *Coucal*'s sailors were alleged to be involved in illegal drug smuggling and distribution activities.

All involved were removed from the ship's company and placed under arrest.

Two of the men were Petty Officers who had ratings difficult to replace on such short notice. Of course, the *Coucal* and the remainder of our crew sailed without replacing them.

Chapter 152

Classified Assignment

A day or two later, I was directed to call on Admiral Small in his office at the Submarine Base.

Upon my arrival, I was ushered in to see him. Following some small talk about the *USS Coucal* and myself, Admiral Small imparted some special instructions to be carried out during our upcoming trip to Japan while on WestPac deployment.

Admiral Small had been captain of the *USS Batfish* (SS-310) during World War II. As such, he made several war patrols. Like some combat veterans, he still held a grudge against the Japanese.

Admiral Small was personally authorizing our ship to call on an island that was recently returned to the Japanese government by the United States. That island was ChiChi Jima.

This is the same island where ten American aviators were shot down by the Japanese during World War II. One of those aviators was rescued at sea by the *USS Finback* (SS-230).

That young Lieutenant was none other than George H. W. Bush, later to become President of the United States. His aircraft was hit by anti-aircraft flak that caused his engine to catch on fire.

Bush completed his bombing mission and then flew several miles from the targeted island, bailing out of his burning TBM Avenger aircraft with another crew member. The other crew member's parachute failed to open, however.

Bush waited four hours in an inflated life raft while Allied fighter planes circled protectively overhead until he could be hauled aboard the lifeguard submarine *Finback*.

Eight of the remaining aviators were captured and held as Prisoners of War in cells on ChiChi Jima. Five of those captured were eventually executed.

Three survivors reported their Japanese captors had eaten the livers of those executed airmen.

Aware of this information, Admiral Small wanted a personal report from me as to what those "blankety-blank sons of Nippon" were now doing on that same island.

Chapter 153

En Route to WestPac

> *"No matter where you travel,*
> *when you meet a guy who's been . . .*
> *There's an instant kind of friendship*
> *'cause we're brothers of the 'phin."*
> **Robert Reed**
> *USS George Washington Carver* (SSBN-656)

After all the training and preparation, it was finally time for the *Coucal* to deploy to the Western Pacific and our temporary home port in Yokosuka, Japan.

We said our goodbyes to family members. Both sides shed some tears as we departed Pearl Harbor en-route to WestPac for a six-month deployment.

As a matter of pride, we departed Pearl Harbor with everything operating up to acceptable standards and nothing on the out of commission list, a first for our ship and its crew.

This was quite a step up from just six months previous when I took command.

While en route, we received orders to change course and head for the remote Pacific Island of Guam.

After two weeks at sea evading the tail-end of a tropical typhoon, we arrived in Guam and moored alongside another submarine tender, the *USS Proteus* (AS-19).

The *Proteus* was a very fine repair ship and submarine tender. They took good care of our almost every need and even assisted us in several small repair items that cropped up during our passage.

It didn't hurt that our Executive Officer Ben Benites had once served as a First Lieutenant aboard the *Proteus* a couple of years prior to him transferring to the *Coucal*.

Chapter 154

Cold War Spy Craft

We were now put under operational control of Commandant of the Fourteenth Naval District and Commander Antisubmarine Warfare Pacific.

We were directed to proceed west of the island of Saipan and to use our divers to investigate what another nation's navy had been doing there just a few weeks before our arrival.

We were to spend two weeks sending divers down at that location.

This area of the Pacific Ocean is known for shallow water and treacherous, uncharted coral reefs that can puncture hulls and sink ships. The charts we had on board showing water depths in the area were very old and none were up to date.

To map the bottom, we used our Fathometer or depth finder constantly as well as an old sailing ship trick.

We lowered one of our anchors to a depth we determined to be a minimum sounding. We then proceeded very slowly until we reached the spot where we were to start our diving operations.

If the exposed anchor were to touch bottom, we had a quick way of knowing we were getting into shallow water. We would then stop and find a new and safer course.

When we arrived at our assigned diving point, we lowered the forward anchor and set it by backing slowly until we were assured it would hold for our entire two-week stay.

We then went to diving stations for the remainder of our operation time.

After exploring the ocean bottom in that area, we discovered as best we could tell that there was a certain group looking for future sites in which to drill for oil.

It was here that we received a terrible scare.

I was in my cabin quietly reading when the general announcing system blared out, "Captain to the Bridge!"

I jumped out of my chair and ran up the steps to the open bridge where the Executive Officer and the Master Diver were engaged in an animated discussion. By their facial expressions, I knew something serious was happening.

Executive Officer Ben Benites reported that two of our divers had failed to surface at the appointed time. At their last known diving location, a three-knot current was detected heading away from the ship.

By this time, the Officer of the Deck had put another one of our work boats in the water.

As a last resort and, on the Executive Officer's suggestion, I directed the Master Diver to get in the boat and follow the current just in case those two divers had been swept away while they were attempting to surface.

The next 15 minutes were the longest I ever spent in my entire Navy career. Many thoughts went crashing through my mind.

What could I possibly say to comfort the families of those two divers if they did not surface? Thank goodness I did not have to do that.

At last, a portable radio on the work boat sounded and the Master Diver reported our two missing divers were found alive and safe.

It seems that in their haste to get into the water for a dive, they had neglected to take along their safety signal flares. That left them with no way to show where and when they surfaced.

We were beyond relief they were now safe, but I was also very irritated with their neglect for training and forgetting their safety equipment.

As you might imagine, they were severely chastised and cautioned to never let the same thing happen again.

Chapter 155

Visit to Saipan

Once we finished this special operation and reported our findings, we requested and were granted a port visit at the island of Saipan.

We arrived there and anchored in the bay adjacent to the city of Garapan. After securing the ship from being at sea and setting the in-port security watches set, liberty for the crew members not currently on duty was granted.

Some members of our crew visited one of the few bars on the island. I accompanied a couple of our officers and stopped by that same bar some hours later for a relaxing drink.

As I was sitting in the bar, an older island native came in and asked whether I was captain of the navy vessel recently anchored in the bay.

"I am," I assured him.

He then offered me a private tour of the island. Naturally, I jumped at this chance.

The old man and I toured the island for nearly three hours. The tour gave me an opportunity to see the large and famous cave where, during World War II, the US MarineCorps caused many Japanese causalities by blowing the cave entrance shut.

Next, my driver showed me Suicide Cliff from which he said the local natives jumped after the Japanese soldiers convinced them that the US Marines would brutalize them and, in particular, their children if they were ever caught.

It has been widely reported that nearly 1,500 adult Chamorros native to Saipan, along with their children, leapt to their deaths from that very cliff.

As we traveled along, we came to a small building beside a graveyard where we stopped and exited the vehicle. As we walked around the adjacent building and grounds, my guide told me this was where the Japanese beheaded the white man.

I had been doing some reading about Amelia Earhart's various flights and the reports of her getting lost back in the 1930s.

I also remembered reading that her navigator was a man by the name of Fred Noonan.

One of the theories yet to be proven as fact is that after Earhart crashed on an island somewhere in that region, the Japanese captured Earhart and Noonan and took them to Saipan for incarceration.

There, they were questioned as suspected spies and eventually the Japanese captors executed Noonan.

Amelia Earhart and Fred Noonan

Earhart, however, was allowed to die in her prison cell.

Next, my driver took me to a very overgrown area where he said there once was a prison.

He pointed to a barred cell at the end of a row of similar spaces.

"That is where they kept the white woman," my driver said.

Back aboard the *Coucal*, I discovered that several of my junior officers had received similar tours and we all had been told identical stories.

I have since checked with one other former officer. His recollections of the private tour he was given matched mine in nearly every detail.

Chapter 156

Mystery of ChiChi Jima

With our special operation for Commander of Antisubmarine Warfare Pacific and our subsequent port visit complete, we departed Saipan and headed as previously directed by Commander Submarines Pacific Admiral Small to the island of ChiChi Jima.

On our approach, we could not help but notice the many areas cut into the hills. These areas were obviously former gun emplacements from World War II. Upon arrival, we had a wonderful port visit and I sent my personal report to Admiral Small detailing all of what I and my officers had observed.

While there, I was given a personal tour of the island and noted the Japanese were turning the island into a recreational and resort area for vacationers from their homeland. It quickly became apparent that ChiChi Jima was and is full of man-made caves dug prior to World War II when Japanese troops occupied these islands. One of those caves is completely copper lined. It was constructed that way for storage of rustable items so they would not deteriorate during long-term storage.

Incidentally, this was my second time to visit ChiChi Jima. While serving in 1956 as a member of the crew on *USS Rock* (SSR-274), we stopped at this same island for a port visit. At that time, the island was under United States control with a Lieutenant Commander Johnson as the Officer in Charge.

During my 1956 visit, our ship's crew played a softball game against the island team. The only difference between then and now was we had won the softball game on my first visit.

There was, however, a very scary event back then as well.

One of the *Rock*'s sailors swam into one of the many shoreline caves as the tide was rising. He became trapped inside the cave for several hours until the tide receded and he was safely able to swim back out without getting battered against the cave walls.

Knowing that the Japanese also loved baseball and softball, we again challenged them to a softball match. This time we lost.

Some said we lost on purpose. Nevertheless, our ship provided the *"Beerou"* — Japanese for beer — for all who attended.

As we were departing the island, we received a flashing light signal. Usually when a ship departs a port, it is a worrisome matter to receive a flashing light signal. The first thing that went through my mind was: What did we do wrong?

This time, though, it was not a problem of any kind. It was just the island softball team sending a farewell thank you for the beer.

"Sayōnara, ōkina sakana," the flashing light signal spelled out In Japanese. Translated into English, the message read, "Good bye you big fish."

We took this message to mean that we were a big hit on the island and that we would be welcomed back there any time.

Chapter 157

Shopping Therapy

Upon arriving in Yokosuka, we reported to Commander Submarine Flotilla Seven who was our operational commander for the remainder of our stay in the Western Pacific.

We also used the Ships Repair Facility as our main repair base while deployed.

During our stay, and thanks in large part to my long-time friend Captain Herb Burton, I had the privilege of briefing Vice Admiral Weisner, Commander of the Seventh Fleet, on our Saipan operations.

I had known Captain Herb Burton from my service time aboard the *USS Pomfret*. Now, however, Captain Burton was the submarine staff officer on Commander Seventh Fleet's staff.

Admiral Weisner later awarded me the Navy Achievement Medal for the Saipan operation and for other evolutions performed by the ship and its crew while we were under his command.

Also during our stay in Yokosuka, we were scheduled for two weeks of general up-keep and repair.

This free time allowed my wife Mary Lou to fly from Hawaii and spend two weeks with the Burtons as we toured some nearby areas of Japan.

Mary Lou was even able to see a stage show, accompanied by some other members of our crew, while visiting in Tokyo.

My wife also spent considerable time visiting a very special Navy Exchange known simply as Building A-32.

Inside, she discovered it was filled with natural wood furniture made with a distinctive Asian flair. This was her favorite place to shop, so shop she did.

Chapter 158

A Close Call

Following two weeks of repairs, it was now time for our ship to depart Yokosuka for Hong Kong where we were to stay one week.

Back then, no nuclear-powered submarine was allowed to visit the port of Hong Kong without another ship capable of towing her back out to sea in case of technical problems. This was the main reason the *Coucal* was making for port at this particular time.

Since Mary Lou was already in Japan, she and I decided this was a prime opportunity for her to visit Hong Kong as well. We went in hock and purchased her air tickets to Hong Kong where she was to meet up with the *Coucal* once we arrived.

Since she was flying, that also gave her four days prior to our arrival when she could shop and enjoy the sights on her own.

During the *Coucal*'s departure from Yokosuka, we were steaming down Sugami Wan at the lower end of Tokyo Bay when we observed a US Navy aircraft carrier several miles ahead of us.

Since aircraft carriers are usually accompanied by a screen of destroyers, we knew this grouping of warships would soon be on our fantail, moving at full speed in order to catch up with the larger and much slower aircraft carrier.

Sure enough, the destroyers came on until they were almost directly behind us and close to being on our rudder.

As they approached our fantail, Executive Officer Ben Benites advised me that we should pull off to the left or right.

I countered by quoting conventional nautical rules of procedure: They were the burdened vessel. We, on the other hand, were required to hold steady on our present course and speed.

"It is the overcoming vessel's duty to maneuver around the slower vessel," I replied.

The destroyers kept coming, however, and very soon they were dangerously close to running us over.

As it was their duty to keep clear of me and my vessel, I grew madder and madder.

The closest ship, a destroyer leader outfitted with guided missiles, finally hauled out to his right in order to clear the *Coucal*. It appeared that the Commanding Officer of that ship was a very senior officer who enjoyed throwing his weight around by threatening the safety of our ship.

As he got closer, I ordered my crew members who were on deck to stand by and we rendered honors to the other ship as it passed very close by our starboard side. Rendering honors involved having our sailors stand at attention and offering a hand salute.

This caught the destroyer's skipper flat-footed as it pointed out to him that he had embarrassed another command on the *Coucal*. It wasn't long before our ship received a flashing light message from the destroyer.

"Captain, you have a smart ship!" was the messaged relayed.

Apparently, that was as close to an apology as we would get.

Chapter 159

Navigating by Braille

We proceeded toward the Taiwan/Formosa Strait and passed close by Sasebo, Japan. This landmark allowed our navigator to take a firm land-based navigational position of our ship at that point.

As it turned out, that would be the last firm position we had until we finally made landfall off the coast of China five days later.

The sky now clouded over and remained so all the way to Hong Kong. That meant there would be no navigating by the stars. To compound matters, the ocean bottom in that area is flat so bottom contour navigating also was of no use.

Additionally, our electronic navigation system — LORAN-A — was useless in this part of the world.

The acronym LORAN is short for long range navigation. This was a system developed in the United States during World War II. It operates at lower frequencies in order to provide improved range up to 1,500 miles with accuracy of plus or minus ten miles.

It was first used for ship convoys crossing the Atlantic Ocean, and then by long-range patrol aircraft. However, its main use was on ships and aircraft operating in the Pacific theatre.

Since we couldn't use LORAN-A, the only way we could determine our position on the charts was a system called D/R. That is where you calculate your ship's position by using the indicated speed of the ship over the ocean's floor as well as the local tide tables.

Our navigator was kept very busy during those five days and nights making the necessary calculations. In fact, he never left the bridge except to answer nature's call for the entire passage.

He even set a cot up on the navigation bridge. A steward would bring his meals up from the pantry.

This was also a politically dangerous period when mainland Chinese Communists and the Chinese Nationalists on Taiwan were engaged in an active war over two little islands, Quemoy and Matsu, located in the Taiwan Strait.

Therefore, it was very important for us to know our position at all times so we would not violate the three-mile territorial limit along the Chinese coastline.

Despite all of these difficulties, our navigator only missed his predicted first sighting of land by 15 minutes. This was a task beyond well done and it was performed faithfully by a very fine and dedicated officer.

Chapter 160

Mystic Hong Kong

We now entered Hong Kong and anchored out in the bay.

This was to be the first of five port visits to Hong Kong by the *Coucal* during this particular WestPac tour.

The reason for our many visits was to accompany all US Navy nuclear submarines so that we could render prompt assistance as well as towing services in case of a serious problem on board one of the boats.

USS Coucal with a submarine alongside

That is also why we remained at anchor out in the bay. We used our work boats as liberty launches and acted as a small submarine tender for minor repairs.

In this manner, we provided liberty launches for numerous submarine crews. We also used our work boats to run errands when they weren't being used as ferry boats to get sailors to shore and back again on board their submarines.

Each of the submarine Commanding Officers were very appreciative of the services we rendered. They kindly thanked us as well as noting our expertise and helpfulness to those further on up the line of command, including our fleet bosses.

Upon our arrival and after making sure everything was operating smoothly, I went ashore to meet up with my wife Mary Lou, who was staying at a hotel in the city of Hong Kong.

During the next several days, she and I spent much of our time together shopping and sightseeing.

I was on a mission to acquire several pairs of "no squeak" shoes. These were beautifully handmade shoes renowned throughout the Far East as quality footwear. Most other shoes were usually fashioned out of green or uncured leather. Once those shoes got wet, they would shrink and start squeaking with every step.

We had also heard about the notorious Wan Chi district of Hong Kong. Mary Lou wanted to go there and see the X-rated red light district avoided by most American tourists and foreign visitors.

This excursion was afforded by a taxi driver who volunteered a visit to his favorite restaurant in that district.

We shared a meal in this restaurant where not one word of English was spoken except by Mary Lou and myself. The only way we could order our meals was by pointing to photographs of each dish printed on the menu.

Since so few foreign visitors frequented this restaurant, the staff honored us by serving our table with a whole fish, cooked complete with its head, eyes, tail and gill flaps still attached.

Afterwards, Mary Lou and I also enjoyed a rare opportunity to visit the famous Tiger Balm Gardens. This was another very famous area of Hong Kong purportedly built by the wealthy owner of the all-healing salve.

Tiger Balm was widely and falsely touted as a cure for any and all ills.

Today, the famous gardens are closed. Visitors can no longer see the house, which was at one time furnished with irreplaceable artifacts such as Ming Dynasty vases and the like. It was certainly something unique for us to see and a memory we will never forget.

That area of Hong Kong has since been restored as a museum.

Chapter 161

Land of the Morning

With our first Hong Kong visit complete and Mary Lou safely on her way back to our boys in Hawaii, the *Coucal* now proceeded to the Philippine Islands, Land of the Morning, and a stop at Subic Bay, then a bustling US Navy base on the outskirts of Manila.

Upon our arrival in the Subic Bay area, the *Coucal* again anchored out in the bay to conduct a few days of deep diver training. Once the training ended, we entered Subic Bay Navy Base proper.

Due to limited docking space, however, we were directed to tie up to a buoy anchored in the inner harbor.

A day or so later, with two-thirds of our crew ashore enjoying liberty, we received an urgent message around midnight from the Senior Officer Present Afloat. The message contained urgent orders for the *Coucal* to get underway immediately.

A small craft was reportedly in serious trouble at sea off the West coast of Luzon, one of the larger islands of the 7,011 that make up that tropical nation. We were ordered to proceed to that area and provide assistance to the disabled boat.

We instituted our emergency recall plan to get our sailors back on board. We needed as many hands as possible so we could function properly while getting underway and operating a rescue at sea.

Thanks to superior training under Executive Officer Ben Benites as well as our other officers and chiefs, the *Coucal* had a large portion of its crew back on board in very short order. In fact, we were underway in less than an hour after receiving orders with 80 percent of our crew on board.

As it turned out, the emergency call for help turned into a false alarm. However, the successful recall of a majority of our crew pointed out the degree to which our training had brought this crew.

As a result, I was one very proud and happy captain.

Chapter 162

Mary Sou's Girls

After leaving Subic Bay, we made our way to the war zone in Viet Nam for another special assignment. When we departed Saigon, we transited back to Yokosuka via the Hainan Island area.

This was a very dangerous part of the South China Sea.

We then detoured and spent some time in and around Taiwan. This included port visits to both Chilung and Kaohsiung. Those were great port visits for our crew.

During our final visit to Hong Kong, we had contracted with the now famous Mary Sou and her girls to chip off our ship's exterior paint and then repaint the entire vessel, both inside and out.

Anticipating this service, prior to leaving Pearl Harbor we sent our Supply Officer, Warrant Officer Jim Gee, and the ship's storekeeper to the Pearl Harbor Ship's Salvage Yard with instructions to commandeer all the brass fittings they could find there.

They were also able to procure quite a bit of old mooring lines that were desired by Mary Sou and her girls.

We also purchased a good quantity of what was then the very newest epoxy paint and stored it on board. At that time, epoxy paint was a revolutionary product and in short supply.

Mary Sou was a legend in Hong Kong. In exchange for our ship's garbage and anything else of value we might offer, she would cause our ship to be completely chipped and painted.

As an added note, when my wife visiting Hong Kong, she was able to meet with Mary Sou. As a friendship gift, Mary Sou gave her a much-treasured practice tablecloth.

This was a beautiful hand-embroidered tablecloth that Mary Sou gives out on very rare occasions. These tablecloths are made by young ladies training to be seamstresses.

Following the chip and paint treatment, the *Coucal* now steamed back to Yokosuka for our final days in WestPac.

We also bid farewell to the Commander Submarine Flotilla Seven's staff, as well as gained some needed pre-voyage repairs prior to heading back to Pearl Harbor, our homes and our loved ones.

Speaking of our loved ones, Mary Lou and some of the wives came up with a grand idea to welcome us back.

Since the *Coucal* and its crew would be spending Christmas in Yokosuka, the wives got together and sewed up more than 85 Christmas stockings.

These were air-shipped to me and I handed out one to each crew member as a Christmas Eve surprise. The stockings were filled with hard candy and a candy cane. This surprise gift went over big and was much appreciated by the crew.

Not to be outdone, our cooks provided a feast on Christmas Day that was something to behold.

Chapter 163

Navy Achievement Medal

Our WestPac trip was rapidly drawing to a close as we departed Japan for the final time during that deployment. Prior to our departure, however, we received a message from Commander United States Seventh Fleet in which Vice-Admiral Weisner awarded me the Navy Achievement Medal. The citation reads:

The Secretary of Navy takes Great Pleasure in Presenting
The Navy Achievement Medal to
Lieutenant Commander James William Gibson,
United States Navy
For service as set forth in the following:

CITATION
"For meritorious Achievement as Commanding Officer of USS Coucal (ASR-8), from 21 September 1970 to 10 February 1971 during operations in the Western Pacific, Lieutenant Commander GIBSON displayed exceptional qualities of leadership while directing his ship in any task assigned.
His personal examples of initiative and devotion to duty inspired his crew to perform at a high level of competence.

Under his outstanding leadership, Coucal remained in a superior material condition throughout this period.

Lieutenant Commander GIBSON's professionalism and devotion to duty reflected great credit upon himself and were in keeping with the highest traditions of the United States Naval Service.

For the Secretary

M.F. WEISNER

Vice Admiral
United States Navy

Chapter 164

Return to Pearl

While en-route home, the crew worked at fever pitch for our arrival in Pearl Harbor. We were fortunate to have smooth seas almost the entire trip. As a result of the good weather and the diligent attention of our crew, the ship arrived spotless with no rust inside or out.

This is a condition not normal for a surface ship after just two or more weeks at sea. Yet, we had been away from our home port for six long months.

We were met and well received by our loved ones who were all waiting for us to tie up at the pier.

It was a joyous occasion. To add to the celebration, Mary Lou and the wives had a very large surprise for us. They had sewn a very large blue and white lei — a traditional Hawaiian floral welcome necklace — for the *Coucal*'s bow.

We were greeted by many dignitaries including the Squadron Commander and Commander Submarine Pacific Rear Admiral Paul Lacy, to whom we presented a *Coucal* baseball cap.

All of these festivities proved to be a grand arrival following a very successful tour of the Western Pacific that including a trip to the Viet Nam war zone.

The ship and crew received the following message:

17 Feb. '71
From: COMSUB PAC
To: USS COUCAL (ASR-8)
Info: COMSUBRON ONE / COMSIBDIV ONE THREE

COUCAL APPEARANCE
On your return from WestPac, the general appearance of COUCAL (ASR-8)l was exemplary. Particularly impressive were the numerous self-help projects that have been completed during the deployment. The order-of-magnitude improvements in the area of habitability attest to the interest and zeal of the commanding officer, who obviously "Cares enough to send the very best to his personnel."
Well done.

Signed: *P.L. Lacy, Jr.*
Rear Admiral,
U.S. Navy

Chapter 165

Relinquishing Command

On Feb. 10, 1971, it was time for me to step down as the *Coucal*'s Commanding Officer. Through some politicking, I managed to have recently promoted Lieutenant Commander Ben Benites, my Executive Officer, relieve me as Commanding Officer of the *Coucal*.

There has never been an officer that deserved it more.

I want to state here and now that Ben Benites was a wonderful Executive Officer and one of the finest Navy officers I ever served with.

It must be pointed out that before the *Coucal*, I had never served on a surface ship. I was certainly qualified as a Commanding Officer of a diesel submarine and I had done much studying and even more research. But I lacked that one intangible item, surface ship experience.

Ben had served on Submarine Rescue Ships for 10 years, off and on. You could reasonably say that he helped and guided me for several months until I got my feet on the deck.

He has since passed on, but he will be missed by all who knew him.

We had a very well attended change of command.

Commander Sam Chesser, then Commander Submariner Division 13, gave the following remarks:

COUCAL CHANGE OF COMMAND:
Admiral Lacy, Commodore Wilson, Commodore Dew, distinguished guests, officers and men of Coucal.

It is my pleasure this morning to spend a few minutes talking to you concerning a rather amazing 17 months in the life of a very fine lady — the USS COUCAL (ASR-8).

She is not as young as some. In fact, at the age of 28, as ships go, she might be considered well past the prime of life.

However, in the past seventeen months, it would appear that she has found the true fountain of youth.

As with good whiskey, Coucal seems to improve with age. Certainly a walk through this ship today would lead you to believe so.

What can this revitalization be attributed to? Certainly the officers and men in Coucal have played a very large part in this — but today, I think it proper to pay tribute to the most important single COG in this or any ship's success or failure — the Commanding Officer, in our case, LCDR James W. Gibson, the Commanding Officer of this fine lady for the past seventeen months. As stated by Joseph Conrad in his writings on Command At Sea:

> *"Only a seaman realizes to what a great extent an entire ship reflects the personality and ability of one individual, her Commanding Officer. To a landsman this is not understandable and sometimes it is even difficult for us to comprehend, but it is so."*

To better understand why I believe this period is worthy of being singled out in the life of this ship, I think a brief recounting of Coucal's recent accomplishments would be appropriate. Fortunately, Coucal has not been called upon to function in her primary role as a submarine rescue vessel. However, there is no doubt that she is fully trained and constantly ready to perform this mission, should the need ever arise.

In her secondary missions of services to other forces and in the special operations that her deep sea diving capability make her uniquely qualified for, she has truly performed in an outstanding manner over the past seventeen months.

In fact, so well that nineteen separate commands felt her performance was worthy of recognition by either originating a letter or message to express their thanks and well dones.

Few ships, new or old, can top that.

Let me give you some examples:

In May 1970, the State of Hawaii recognized Coucal's efforts in the "Crown of Thorns" starfish eradication project as follows;

> *Our recently concluded starfish eradication project was an unqualified success with the destruction of over 9,600 starfish. In large measure this success was due to the assignment of the USS Coucal (ASR-8) as an on-scene diver support ship and magnificent cooperation extended by LCDR James Gibson and all the personnel aboard the Coucal. I am convinced that without the Coucal's stable platform upon which the divers could rest and without her tank recharging capabilities, the eradication program of the intensity attempted would not have been possible.*

*Particularly gratifying was this positive
demonstration that the military and civilian
counterparts could and do work so well together.
Please accept the heart-felt thanks of the State of
Hawaii, as well as my own for the tremendous
assistance and a job exceedingly well executed.*

Sincerely,
Sunao Kido
*Chairman and Member
Board of Land and Natural Resources*

Earlier this month, Coucal received notification
that she had been awarded the Meritorious Unit
Commendation for Special Operations conducted
for Com-ASW-For-Pac in March 1970.

A just-completed WestPac tour was a complete
success. Coucal met every commitment and on
time.

In the course of this deployment, an impressive
number of "self-help" projects were completed,
resulting in order-of-magnitude improvement in
many areas — particularly in the habitability area
of the crew's mess, berthing spaces and lounge
area.

The crew accomplished these "self-help" projects
while still maintaining this operating ship in near
4.0 mechanical-condition.

In fact, I think the overall appearance of Coucal
today is better than that of any ASR I have seen in
the eighteen years that I have been observing
submarine rescue vessels.

The identity of the fountain of youth for Coucal
lies in the people responsible for these "self-help"
projects — namely, a dedicated crew and a
commanding officer whose interest, zeal and high
standards have been the inspiration, for these
improvements.

In our drive towards a people orientated Navy, where does this lady stand?

I think it is safe to say, if every Command Officer stood up for and looked out for his crew with the same zeal as LCDR Gibson, many of the problems facing the Navy today would not exist.

Coucal, in the past six months ,has reenlisted more men on board than were reenlisted on Coucal in the preceding four years. She just completed a six month tour in WESTPAC without receiving a single shore patrol report.

I have found the morale on this ship to be extremely high and the identification of the crew with the ship to exceed every expectation.

Jim, you and Coucal have had a remarkable and enviable association.

Your inspiration and leadership has been the primary ingredient in this fine lady's "Fountain of Youth" and will not be shortly forgotten. As you go up to join the Staff of COMSUBPAC, you and your

Ben Benites, right, relieves James Gibson as *Coucal's* captain

333

lovely family carry with you our best wishes for continued success.

Following those remarks by Sam Chesser, Lieutenant Ben Benites relieved me with the same words I had used just 17 months before.

"I relieve you, Sir!" he said before rendering a smart 45-degree hand salute to the brim of his cap.

Chapter 166

Kudos All Around

Shortly after returning to Pearl Harbor from our WestPac trip, I sat down with my Executive Officer and the ship's other officers to form an awards board.

Jointly, we recommended several awards to be considered for various members of our crew. These awards ranged from the Navy Commendation Medal down to a Letter of Commendation from the Division Commander.

Several officers higher up the chain of command than expressed concerns that I was abusing the awards system by giving out too many decorations, citations and commendations.

By using behind-the-scenes sources, I made sure that those same officers knew exactly from where the *Coucal* had arrived in just 17 short months as well as why the ship was presently able to be in such superb condition.

A great amount of credit was bestowed on me, but none of this would have been possible were it not for my wonderful crew, a great group of Chief Petty Officers, and a wardroom consisting of the most dedicated Navy officers with whom I ever had the pleasure to serve.

Not one of the decorations given out was overstated.

In reality, in many cases they were much less than what the individuals so recognized actually deserved.

The awards board was conducted during my last day on board, and the recommendations forwarded even as I departed the *USS Coucal*.

Chapter 167

Old Man and the Sea

"Let the blessing of St. Peter's Master be . . .
upon all that are lovers of virtue; and dare trust in His
providence; and be quiet; and go a-Angling."
Author **Isaak Walton**
The Compleat Angler, Chapter 21

Immediately following that final day, I invited my father, who had come to Hawaii for a visit and to stay with us for a few weeks, on a fishing excursion with a few of my crew members.

Chief Petty Officer Kerr set up a fishing trip using the Submarine Base Recreation's off-shore fishing boat.

Along with the Chief and another sailor on board, Dad and I proceeded to go out past the entrance to Pearl Harbor to try our luck at deep-sea fishing.

At the beginning of our excursion, the four of us each drew straws to establish the order in which we would pick up one of the poles whenever we encountered a strike on the line.

Thus fate decided that Dad was to be second in line. A sailor named La Bar was to be first.

Alas, La Bar lost his fish.

Now it was Dad's turn.

There was a second strike and a fish was on the line. We helped my father into the fighting chair and a mighty battle between man and fish ensued.

The fish Dad had on his hook turned out to be a very large Mahi Mahi. Dad commented while fighting the sea creature that the most recent fish he had previously caught was a 6-inch chub taken from a little creek back home when he was just 6 years old.

Now, he was 74 and somewhat frail. Dad was fighting this big fish and doing a good job. I leaned over his shoulder for moral support.

"Jim, help me!" he said.

"You caught it. You land it," I responded with a grin, but I was ready to quickly step in if I noticed him weakening in any way.

He continued on with the struggle and eventually he did win the mighty battle.

When we arrived back in port, we paraded Dad and his catch down to the *Coucal*, where he proudly showed off his 45 pound Mahi Mahi.

When any of the *Coucal*'s crew members would pass by on the stern of the ship, he would ask each of them to take his picture.

Several photos were taken and some of them ended up decorating a poster board back at his home church in Mount Jackson, Penn.

Chapter 168

Standing Watch

A few days after leaving the *Coucal*, I reported to the Operations Section of Command Submarines Pacific where I was assigned to be a Command Center Watch Officer.

This entailed being on duty for eight hours at a time, along with a senior enlisted man. Both of us would be armed. It was our job to monitor the movement of all submarines under ComSubPac's purview.

Our main task was to be responsible for confirming information coming from senior commanders if and when the ballistic submarines were ever required — God help us — to launch their missiles.

We also had to be on the alert for any practice or test messages that would allow the entire system, from the top all the way down to the submarines at sea, to correct any readiness problems.

This was a very stressful job.

Also during this time, I was coaching the ComSubPac's softball team. That was lots of fun.

When the sports season changed, I was also the officer representative for the SubPac basketball team. I even had an opportunity to travel with the SubPac basketball team to Norfolk, Va, where we participated in an All-Navy tournament.

The tournament went well and our team brought home a second-place trophy.

After about a year of this desk job, however, I had enough of this very stressful watch standing and asked to be relieved.

The two-and-a-half years we spent in Hawaii proved a wonderful bonding time for our entire family.

There was so much to do and see.

The command base offered 25-cent movies and the boys were able to do lots of surfing and sail boating on nearby beaches. Both boys were also able to make some money by washing dishes at the submarine base mess hall.

Coach, ComSubPac softball team

Mary Lou and I would take the boys to the beach at Barber's Point whenever I was off duty

Mary Lou was also very involved with the other Navy wives. Overall, the time we spent in Hawaii was quite enjoyable.

Chapter 169

Meritorious Service Medal

During this tour, I was awarded the Meritorious Service Medal for my performance as Commanding officer of *USS Coucal* (ASR 8).

The President of the United States takes pleasure in presenting the

MERITORIOUS SERVICE MEDAL
to
Lieutenant Commander James W. GIBSON
United states Navy
For service as set forth in the following

CITATION

"For meritorious conduct in the performance of outstanding service as Commanding Officer, USS COUCAL (ASR-8) from 12 October 1969 to 27 February 1971.
An extremely professional and energetic leader, Lieutenant Commander GIBSON was responsible for the administration, operational training and material readiness of his ship.
In discharging these responsibilities, he essentially rebuilt and revitalized his ship both from the personnel and material standpoint.

The present high standard attained and successful performance of his ship reflects the outstanding quality of his professional abilities. Under his leadership, every operational commitment assigned to COUCAL was met.

His exemplary performance was highlighted by the outstanding spirit, morale and attitudes of personnel in his crew who were inspired to maximum performance by his enthusiasm, warmth and personal leadership.

Lieutenant Commander GIBSON's outstanding professional skill and inspiring devotion to duty were in keeping with the highest traditions of the United States Naval Service

For the President

Vice Admiral Nels C. Johnson

Commander First Fleet

Supporting documents for the award:

Lieutenant Commander Gibson assumed command of USS COUCAL (ASR-8), in October 1969 when the ship was at the lowest ebb of her life cycle. Ship morale was extremely low, the crew was poorly trained and the material readiness was insufficient to support any long deployment.

He quickly diagnosed the problems at hand and energetically set out to remedy them.

Recognizing that personnel operate best under a well thought-out and sound administrative organization, LCDR GIBSON laid out a new organization manual for ASR's, the current SSORM now in common use by ASR's in the Pacific Fleet.

He then directed and personally supervised the rewriting of the Ship's Instructions and

Departmental Orders which were so outdated that the departments were unable to utilize them effectively to carry out their responsibilities.

He initiated a shipboard training plan containing the "Fast Cruise System" used by submarines for team training prior to getting underway.

He supervised the revision of the training status instruction and devised a reporting system which aligned ASRs with the other ships in SUBPAC so that higher echelons of command could readily recognize the training requirements necessary to allow ASRs to operate efficiently.

One of the initial indications of improved morale on Coucal became evident in December 1969 when the ship, through extensive crew imagination and participation, won the award for the "best decorated ship" in the Pearl Harbor area during the Christmas season.

In January 1970, Coucal was assigned to Fleet Training Group for refresher training.

LCDR GIBSON continued his effort to upgrade ship performance by taking maximum advantage of this training opportunity.

Commander Fleet Training Group Pearl Harbor reported that Coucal "was the most cooperative ship they had trained in three years."

Coucal achieved the highest gunnery score in the Pacific Fleet. Coucal was then assigned to COMASWFORPAC for a mission of great value to the government of the United States.

The successful completion of this mission resulted in the awarding of the Meritorious Unit Commendation to Coucal.

Coucal then began preparations for the WESTPAC deployment scheduled to commence in October 1970.

Through preplanning and imaginative foresight used by the Commanding Officer to insure

The Meritorious Service Medal was awarded in the name of the President of the United States by Vice Admiral Nels C. Johnson Commander First Fleet, on 4 June 1971.

Chapter 170

Navy Recruiting Officer

Upon completion of my tour in the operations section of Commander Submarine Force Pacific, I was ordered to the Naval Recruiting Command inAlbuquerque, New Mexico.

My assignment was Officer in Charge of the Navy Recruiting A Station in El Paso, Texas.

After our family said its goodbyes and farewells to all of our friends there in Hawaii at a party or two, the family flew from Hawaii to San Francisco.

Once again, Mary Lou and the boys spent some time with Mary Lou's parents while waiting for our automobile and Dachshund puppy to arrive from Hawaii.

During this time, I had to report to Recruiting Officer Management Orientation in Pensacola, Florida.

This three week course was to prepare future officer recruiters on how to properly deal with the general public.

My orientation course included an introduction to the history and philosophy of the Navy Recruiting Command; the high priority given to the recruiting effort; as well as the management responsibilities of a recruiting officer in the field.

Human relations, motivation and the application of empathy in recruiting were also introduced as topics of study.

Classroom instruction also dealt with the programs available to applicants such as the use of visual aids and other tools of the "recruiter-salesman."

The procedures for applicant processing, interview techniques and the dignity and necessity of selling in a competitive market environment was also stressed.

Individual participation was encouraged through role playing techniques in the classroom and public speaking at a Toastmasters "Gavel Club" luncheon each working day.

After successfully completing this course, the following citation was presented.

CITATION

LCDR Gibson actively and enthusiastically participated in every phase of this short, but intensive course. LCDR Gibson was selected by his peers for the "Something Special Award." This honor is bestowed on the individual who, in the consensus of the class, demonstrated the greatest potential for success in recruiting.

Signed: *William C Dixon*
Captain, United States Navy

347

Chapter 171

Puppy Smuggling

Throughout my entire Navy career, we enjoyed the wonderful support that Mary Lou's parents provided our family. It was reassuring to know we could call on them at a moment's notice.

They could be counted on and were always eager to back us up by offering us a place to stay until we could get settled elsewhere.

Upon leaving Vallejo, we drove across the desert southwest to El Paso, Texas, after stopping for a day in Albuquerque, NM, whereupon I reported in to the Commander, Navy Recruiting Command.

We stayed overnight in transitional officer's housing at Kirkland Air Force Base. During our stay, a cute thing happened.

Since no pets was the rule for these in-transit officer's quarters, we were in a quandary of what to do with our pet Dachshund.

We couldn't just leave our much adored and pampered animal in the car. We finally solved this problem by placing the dog in one of our empty suitcases and carrying him up to our room.

He was so well-behaved that no one was the wiser, but this act of smuggling our doggie into our hotel room did leave a lasting impression on the little fellow.

I don't think he has gone anywhere near a suitcase ever since.

Chapter 172

Making a Name for the Navy

We arrived in El Paso and, after a week of house hunting and getting the family settled, I reported to the Naval Recruiting "A" Station to inform my bosses up the line that I was present and in charge.

My office responsibilities included overseeing the work of two other officers, several senior Petty Officers and a small clerical staff.

Together, we laid out the ground work to properly administer the many recruiters in various cities and towns in the vast area surrounding El Paso.

Our territory extended west to Las Cruces, New Mexico, and as far east as Big Springs, Texas. Our northern-most city was Amarillo, and to the south we had responsibility for all of the remainder of Texas down to the southern border with Mexico.

This was an interesting assignment.

When I received orders to report to El Paso, I found out I had a friend — Captain and later Rear Admiral Lando Zeck — who was the number two person in the US Naval Recruiting Command in Washington, DC. El Paso was and is the home of Fort Bliss, one of the largest US Army bases in the entire United States.

Captain Zeck instructed me to make the Navy known and prominent in this Army town. In fact, he told me that was my primary duty.

This started me on a round-robin of civic events for the next two years.

Thankfully, I had learned from my previous command that when you have a problem, the best way to start to solve it is call on your Chief Petty Officers.

I called the local recruiters in and asked each of them what we could do to get more involved in the happenings of the city and its surrounding area. They informed me that the biggest social event of the year was always the Sun Bowl, a football game and community celebration that was coming up soon on the calendar.

They next introduced me to several very prominent and leading citizens, the so-called City Fathers.

With some help from a local Naval Reserve Unit, we entered every large event from the Sun Bowl Parade to serving as ushers at the Sun Bowl football game. Also at the football game, we invited a training squadron from the Naval Air Station at Beeville, Texas, to thrill the crowd with a close-by military fly over.

This was quite a thing. They coordinated their timing in flight overhead to perform a Missing Man formation just as Lynn Anderson was completing her rendition of the Star Spangled Banner.

I do not believe there was one dry eye remaining in that entire stadium.

The Navy went all out to support us. One year we had a Wave's drill team come out from Pensacola, Florida, for one of the Sun Bowl's parades. We had the Navy's steel drum band from San Juan, Porto Rico, perform at the city's downtown event center.

In May 1973, we invited the Navy's premier flight team, the Blue Angels, to perform for a large crowd in El Paso. Following their performance, the Blue Angels flight crews honored Mary Lou and I by visiting our home for a sit-down dinner with some of the community members who were instrumental in our recruiting efforts as well as the Navy-sponsored events.

Through the local professional baseball team's efforts, we sponsored a Navy Night at the ball park. As a result, some of our sailors were asked to sit on the home team's bench. There, they met with several future Major League ballplayers.

We also were able to meet an MLB Hall of Fame player, Lefty Gomez, formerly with the New York Yankees, who happened to be in the area visiting a friend.

I quickly learned that El Paso, Texas, is one of the most patriotic cities in the nation.

I could go to one end of the town with a drum and a bugle and start walking towards the other end of town. Before I was to the half-way point, I would have 1,000 people marching in step in my parade and another 5,000 people lining the sidewalks to watch.

This was a very enjoyable spot for my family as well. I was the senior Navy officer in the area, so Mary Lou and I were invited to a great many city functions and social gatherings in the area.

We met and made a great many friends and built long-lasting friendships that have endured throughout the years.

Our time in El Paso was declared a great success when our tour there ended once I requested placement on the US Navy Officers Corps' Retired List.

Thanks to the US Navy Reserve Unit, there was a formal retirement parade held in my honor with now-Rear-Admiral Lando Zeck flying out from Washington, DC., to participate and present me with the Navy Commendation Medal.

Chapter 173

Epilogue

Thus ended my 26-year career in the United States Navy that began July 7, 1948, in Mount Jackson, a small town in Western Pennsylvania.

I was still a young kid when I raised my right hand and swore an oath to be part of the defense system for the United States of America.

Whether it was from hard work, the love and attention of my adoptive parents, our shared faith in God, the Navy's diligence in training young men and women for thoughtful service to country, setting lofty personal goals or maintaining a high bar of excellence for myself or others, somehow or other every project I tackled, every job I was assigned, every opportunity I faced turned out golden.

Except for a few notable exceptions detailed in this book.

Some have even claimed I had the proverbial Midas touch.

I would not go that far, but I do know this to be true.

Most of my subsequent career would never have happened if it were not for the love and affection of a wonderful young woman, Mary Louise (Lou) Buckthought, a native of Grass Valley, California, who early on agreed to be my wife and partner for life.

Mary Lou was and continues to be a very attentive mother who almost single-handedly at times raised our two fine sons, sometimes with little or no money, while I was off doing Navy things.

I am also very proud of our two fine sons Bill and Rich, who have successfully pursued their own careers.

Last, but certainly not least, I owe a deep debt of heartfelt thanks to my parents, Sam and Sarah Belle Gibson, two very dedicated and hard-working people who took a chance and adopted me, a mere infant, in 1931.

Brought together by an oath united by a common thread

I first met Lieutenant Commander Jim Gibson in 1997 at a United States Submarine Veterans Incorporated (USSVI) Mare Island Base meeting, which he subsequently joined. Our chance acquaintanceship developed into a long and very interesting friendship.

This started well before I knew much about Jim's storied Navy career. I have had the pleasure of following Jim's exploits for the past 20 years.

Jim has proven to be the epitome Energizer Bunny when it comes to veterans, especially submarine veterans and veteran-related community programs throughout Northern California.

For example, Jim helped organize and establish the Cuttlefish Base of USSVI in Redding, Calif., and served as its first base commander.

Jim is also a member of the International Submarine Association. He has participated at several international conventions fostering goodwill with submariners from various countries.

Jim has chaired several committees resulting in the establishment of numerous veteran memorials and monuments throughout Shasta County, including the forthcoming Northern California Veterans Museum & Heritage Center being created and established in Anderson, Calif.

Jim also spends at least one day a week at the Northern California Veterans Cemetery in Igo, Calif., assisting at graveside and inurnment niche services along with Missing In America Project and Patriot Guard Riders.

Jim is also active with other veteran groups such as Veterans of Foreign Wars, American Legion and AmVets.

He serves on several governing boards for these various veterans groups including the Northern California Veterans Home Support Committee.

Sincerely,

Dom Boncore